Mary E Wilder

The Study of History

By the Laboratory Method, for High and Grammar Schools. England

Mary E Wilder

The Study of History
By the Laboratory Method, for High and Grammar Schools. England

ISBN/EAN: 9783744777377

Printed in Europe, USA, Canada, Australia, Japan

Cover: Foto ©Paul-Georg Meister /pixelio.de

More available books at **www.hansebooks.com**

THE
STUDY OF HISTORY

BY THE

LABORATORY METHOD

FOR

HIGH AND GRAMMAR SCHOOLS

𝔈𝔫𝔤𝔩𝔞𝔫𝔡

BY

MARY E. WILDER

LEE AND SHEPARD PUBLISHERS
10 MILK STREET
BOSTON
1895

COPYRIGHT, 1891, 1894, BY MARY E. WILDER

———

All Rights Reserved

———

STUDY OF ENGLISH HISTORY

ELECTROTYPED BY C. J. PETERS & SON
PRESSWORK BY S. J. PARKHILL & CO.
BOSTON MASS.

PREFACE

The following topical arrangement was prepared for my own use in classes in the Gloucester High School. Because of the immaturity of the pupils no attempt was made to bring out the weightier side of English History. Hence the deeper constitutional and ecclesiastical subjects were avoided, and it has been thought unwise to depart from the original plan in offering the work to the public.

At the end of each period I have inserted a short list of historical novels and dramas, as they give us a picture of manners and customs usually lacking in the history proper.

The following is a list of the authorities referred to in these topics. The name of the author only is given, except when more than one work of a writer is referred to.

J. J. Anderson . . .	School Hist. of England . . .	*Ma.*
Mrs. E. S. Armitage	The Childhood of Eng. Nation	*Longm.*
Grant Allen	Anglo-Saxon Britain	*Soc. Ch. K.*
J. F. Bright	Eng. Hist. for use of Pub. Schools	4 *vols. D.*
A. J. Church	Story of Early Britain . . .	*Put.*
A. J. Church	Henry V.	*Macm. E. M. A.*
B. M. Cordery and J. S. Phillpotts	King and Commonwealth . .	*C.*
M. Creighton . . .	The Age of Elizabeth	*Scr. E. S.*
M. Creighton . . .	Wolsey	*Macm. T. E. S.*
E. S. Creasy	Fifteen Decisive Battles . . .	*H.*
Chas. Dickens . . .	The Child's History of Eng. .	*H. & M.*
E. A. Freeman . . .	Old English History	*Macm.*
E. A. Freeman . . .	Hist. of the Norman Conquest	6 *vols. Macm.*
E. A. Freeman . . .	Shorter Hist. of the Norman Conquest	*Macm.*

E. A. Freeman	William the Conqueror	*Macm. T. E. S.*
J. A. Froude	Hist. of Eng. from Fall of Wolsey to Death of Elizabeth	12 *vols. Scr.*
S. R. Gardiner	Student's History of England	*Longm.*
S. R. Gardiner	The Puritan Revolution	*Scr. E. S.*
J. Gairdner	Henry VII	*Macm. T. E. S.*
J. Gairdner	The Houses of Lancaster and York	*Scr. E. S.*
J. R. Green	The Conquest of England	*H.*
J. R. Green	The Making of England	*H.*
J. R. Green	History of the English People	4 *vols. H.*
J. R. Green	Sh. Hist. of the Eng. People	*H.*
Mrs. J. R. Green	Henry II	*Macm. T. E. S.*
F. Guizot	History of English Revolution	*B.*
E. Hale	The Fall of the Stuarts	*Scr. E. S.*
F. Harrison	Oliver Cromwell	*Macm. T. E. S.*
Thomas Hughes	Alfred the Great	*Macm.*
David Hume	Hist. of Eng. Student's Ed.	*H.*
W. Hunt	Norman Britain	*Soc. Ch. K.*
S. O. Jewett	The Story of the Normans	*Put.*
A. H. Johnson	The Normans in Britain	*Scr.*
C. Knight	The Popular Hist. of England	*S.*
T. M. Lappenberg	The English under the Anglo-Saxon Kings	2 *vols. B.*
W. E. H. Lecky	Hist. of England in the 18th Century	4 *vols. App.*
J. Lingard	History of England	13 *vols. Shea.*
T. B. Macaulay	History of England	5 *vols. Dell. & P.*
J. McCarthy	History of our own Times	2 *vols. H.*
J. McCarthy	Epoch of Reform	*Scr.*
J. McCarthy	Four Georges	4 *vols. H.*
Robert MacKenzie	19th Century	*N.*
H. Martineau	History of England	*B.*
C. E. Moberly	The Early Tudors	*Scr. E. S.*
D. H. Montgomery	The Leading Facts of English History	*Ginn.*
E. E. Morris	The Age of Anne	*Scr. E. S.*
E. E. Morris	The Early Hanoverians	*Scr. E. S.*
C. W. Oman	Warwick	*Macm. E. M. A.*
H. M. Scarth	Roman Britain	*Soc. Ch. K.*

W. Stubbs	The Early Plantagenets	*Scr. E. S.*
A. Thierry	The Norman Conquest	2 *vols. B.*
G. M. Towle	Young People's Hist. of Eng.	*L. and S.*
G. M. Towle	Young People's Hist. of Ire.	*L. and S.*
H. D. Traill	William III	*Macm. T. E. S.*
W. Warburton	Edward III	*Scr. E. S.*
A. H. Welsh	Development of Eng. Lit. and Lang.	*G.*
A. M. Wheeler	Sketches from English History	*Ch.*
C. M. Yonge	Cameos from English History	7 *vols. Macm.*

In the abbreviations, App. stands for Appleton; B. for Bell (Bohn Library); C. for Coates; Ch. for Chautauqua; DeW. & F. for DeWolfe, Fiske & Co.; D. for Dutton; G. for Griggs & Co.; H. for Harper; H. & M. for Houghton, Mifflin & Co.; L. and S. for Lee and Shepard; Longm. for Longmans; M. for Maynard; Macm. for MacMillan; N. for Nelson; Put. for Putnam; S. for Sangster; Scr. for Scribner; Soc. Ch. K. for Society for Promoting Christian Knowledge; E. S. for Epoch Series; E. M. A. for English Men of Action; T. E. S. for Twelve English Statesmen.

ADDITIONAL AND MISCELLANEOUS LIST

W. H. D. Adams	Battle Stories from English History.
Lucy Aiken	Memoirs of the Court of Queen Elizabeth.
Osmund Airy	The English Restoration and Louis XIV.
Thomas Arnold	Modern England.
E. S. Beesly	Elizabeth.
Oscar Browning	Modern England.
J. Corbett	Drake.
G. W. Cox	The Crusades.
Mrs. M. Creighton	England a Continental Power.
M. Creighton	The Tudors and the Reformation.
M. Creighton	Life of Marlborough.
G. P. Fisher	The Reformation.
B. M. Gardiner	Struggle against Absolute Monarchy.
T. W. Higginson	History of England for American Readers.
Longmans	Summary of English History.
T. B. Macaulay	Essays.
Charles Norris	Historical Tales.

Preface

C. W. Oman	Warwick.
C. H. Pearson	English History of the 14th Century.
G. W. Prothero	Simon de Montford.
L. von Ranke	History of England.
W. J. Rolfe	Tales from English History in Prose and Verse.
James Rowley	Rise of the People and Growth of Parliament.
James Rowley	Settlement of the Constitution.
Frederic Seebohm	The Era of the Protestant Revolution.
Agnes Strickland	Lives of the Queens of England.
O. W. Tancock	England during American and European Wars.
W. M. Thackeray	Four Georges.
F. F. Tout	Edward I.
G. M. Towle	Drake the Sea-King.
G. M. Towle	Raleigh: His Exploits and Voyages.
A. Waites	Historical Student's Manual.
Sir Chas. Wilson	Clive.
F. York-Powell	Early England.
C. M. Yonge	History of England.
C. M. Yonge	Stories from English History for Young People.

MINIMUM LIST FOR TOPICS

Armitage	Childhood of the English Nation.
Bright	English History for Use of Public Schools.
Church	Story of Early Britain.
Freeman	Shorter History of the Norman Conquest.
Gardiner	Student's History of England.
Green	History of the English People.
Green	Shorter History of the English People.
Hughes	Alfred the Great.
Hume	Student's Edition of History of England.
Knight	Popular History of England.

MARY E. WILDER.

GLOUCESTER, *September*, 1894.

HINTS TO TEACHERS

THOSE inexperienced in the use of the laboratory method will find the following hints of assistance.

These topics form a network which the teacher must take care to fill in with solid work adapted to the capacity of the pupil. It is worth while to insist on the memorizing of the topics.

Note-books are necessary, and two are not too many; one for notes taken in the class from the teacher or other pupils; the other for the student's own personal researches. If the pupil is very immature, he should be guided for a time in choice of material for his note-book.

He should be encouraged to consult two or more authorities on all topics, and to read continuously some history other than those used for reference; likewise to own at least one, the best he can afford.

Atlases should be in constant use, and progressive maps should be prepared by the pupil, subject to examination by the teacher from time to time.

Essays written on subjects connected with the study are helpful. This work may be varied by writing a review of some historical novel which has been read as a part of the prescribed work.

Historical novels, scrap-books for cuttings and pictures, the learning of spirited poems and ballads, all help to rouse the interest and enthusiasm.

A library of books of reference is necessary to the successful use of the laboratory method. But one need not depend on public funds for such supplies. Schools and classes can by a little effort obtain these for themselves. Our own school owns not far from twelve hundred volumes, nearly all of which were bought by the school with money earned in lecture courses and entertainments.

ENGLISH HISTORY

ANCIENT ENGLAND.

Montgomery, 1-2.

Original Inhabitants:

**Character,
Government,
Mode of Life,
Religion.**

{ Armitage, 4, 5.
Church, 1-10.
Dickens, 1-5.
Freeman, 1-12.
Gardiner, i. 1-10.
Hume, 2-6.
Knight, i. 12, 13.
Lappenberg, i. 2-17.
Lingard, i. 7-19.
Scarth, 7-15. }

ROMAN CONQUESTS.   55 B.C.–449 A.D.

Montgomery, 12-30.   Anderson, 15-27.   Towle, 1-11.

Invasions:

Cæsar,

{ Armitage, 5-7.
Church, 12-30.
Dickens, 5, 6.
Freeman, 12-14.
Gardiner, i. 10-12.
Hume, 7, 8.
Knight, i. 2-12.
Lappenberg, i. 22-27.
Lingard, i. 1-6, 19, 20.
Scarth, 20-34. }

English History

Emperor Claudius, Plautius,
- Church, 31-38.
- Dickens, 6.
- Freeman, 15.
- Gardiner, i. 12-14.
- Hume, 8, 9.
- Knight, i. 16-21.
- Lappenberg, i. 28-32.
- Lingard, i. 20-25.
- Scarth, 35-45.

Suetonius, Attack on Druids, Revolt of Boadicea,
- Church, 48-57.
- Dickens, 7.
- Freeman, 16.
- Gardiner, i. 14, 15.
- Hume, 9.
- Knight, i. 22-26.
- Lappenberg, i. 28-35.
- Lingard, i. 26, 27.
- Scarth, 46-54.

Government of Agricola,
- Church, 58-65.
- Dickens, 7, 8.
- Freeman, 17-19.
- Gardiner, i. 16, 17.
- Hume, 10.
- Knight, i. 26-29.
- Lappenberg, i. 36-39.
- Lingard, i. 27-31.
- Scarth, 57-65.

Wall of Hadrian,
- Church, 66-74.
- Freeman, 20.
- Gardiner, i. 17-19.
- Hume, 11.
- Knight, i. 29, 30.
- Lingard, i. 36, 37.
- Scarth, 66-68, 73-78.

Severus,
- Church, 76-78.
- Freeman, 20.
- Gardiner, i. 19.
- Hume, 11.

Severus, (*Continued.*)	Knight, i. 29-31. Lappenberg, i. 52, 53. Lingard, i. 38-42. Scarth, 88-92.
Roads, Forts, Language, Religion.	Dickens, 9. Freeman, 20, 21. Gardiner, i. 19-23. Green, Making of Eng., 3, 4. Hume, 13-15. Knight, i. 32-38. Lappenberg, i. 44, 45, 59-61, 64-67, 81-85. Lingard, i. 47. Scarth, 114-123, 159, 160. Wheeler, 25-30.

CHURCH: *The Count of the Saxon Shore.*
EBERS: *The Emperor.*
HENTY: *Beric the Briton.*
SHAKESPEARE: *Julius Cæsar.*

ENGLISH CONQUEST. 449 A.D.–1066 A.D.

Montgomery, 31-57.   Anderson, 28-69.   Towle, 11-57.

Settlements,
- Allen, 1-8, 23-25.
- Armitage, 8, 9, 11.
- Bright, i. 1, 2.
- Church, 94-111.
- Dickens, 11-13.
- Freeman, 22-41.
- Freeman, Sh. Hist. of Nor. Conq., 7.
- Gardiner, i. 26-28.
- Green, Eng. Peo., i. 22-31.
- Green, Sh. Hist., 7-16.
- Green, Making of Eng., 44-52.
- Hume, 21-28.
- Knight, i. 63.
- Lappenberg, i. 115-126.
- Lingard, i. 60-73.

King Arthur,
- Bulfinch, Age of Chivalry.
- Church, 100.
- Cox, Popular Romances.
- Freeman, 35, 36.
- Gardiner, i. 33, 34.
- Hume, 27.
- Lappenberg, i. 129-131.

Character of Conquest,
King,
Government,
- Armitage, 9, 10, 12-17, 34-41.
- Gardiner, i. 28-37, 44, 45.
- Green, Eng. Peo., i. 30-36, 93.
- Green, Sh. Hist., 9-16.
- Green, Conquest of Eng., 32-37.
- Hume, 70-76.
- Lingard, i. 79, 80, 99-101.
- Wheeler, 30-35.

English Conquest 13

Coming of Christianity,
Gregory,
Augustine,
- Allen, 85-92.
- Armitage, 18-23, 26, 27.
- Bright, i. 3, 4.
- Church, 120-131.
- Dickens, 13.
- Freeman, Old Eng. Hist., 42-50.
- Freeman, i. 19-23.
- Gardiner, i. 38-40.
- Green, Eng. Peo., i. 37, 38, 40-42.
- Green, Sh. Hist., 17, 18.
- Green, Making of Eng., 201-210.
- Hume, 30, 31.
- Knight, i. 64-69.
- Lappenberg, i. 171-175.
- Lingard, i. 75-97.
- Thierry, i. 28-33.
- Wheeler, 35-39.

Cædmon,
- Allen, 209, 210.
- Armitage, 25.
- Church, 151-155.
- Gardiner, i. 51, 52.
- Green, Eng. Peo., i. 54, 55.
- Green, Sh. Hist., 27-29.
- Green, Making of Eng., 357, 358.
- Hughes, 19-21.
- Hume, 35, 77.

Bæda,
- Allen, 61, 109-112, 213.
- Church, 157-161.
- Freeman, 74.
- Gardiner, i. 52.
- Green, Eng. Peo., i. 64-67.
- Green, Sh. Hist., 38-40.
- Green, Making of Eng., 383-390.
- Lappenberg, i. 265-266.
- Lingard, i. 113, 114.

Egbert, King of the English, 828,
- Allen, 120-124, 131.
- Armitage, 42-44.
- Bright, i. 5.
- Church, 180-184.
- Dickens, 14, 15.

Egbert, King of the English, 828,
(Continued.)

> Freeman, i. 27-33.
> Freeman, Old Eng. Hist., 95-106.
> Gardiner, i. 54, 55.
> Green, Sh. Hist., 42-44.
> Green, Eng. Peo., i. 71, 72.
> Hughes, 32, 33, 40-43.
> Hume, 34, 36, 39, 40.
> Knight, i. 75-79.
> Lappenberg, ii. 1-12.
> Lingard, i. 143-146.

ALFRED.   871–901.

Childhood, Youth,

> Allen, 136.
> Armitage, 45, 46.
> Church, 199-202.
> Dickens, 16.
> Freeman, Old Eng. Hist., 113-116.
> Green, Conquest of Eng., 94-96.
> Hughes, 34-37, 47-55.
> Knight, i. 82-85.
> Lappenberg, ii. 29, 30, 50-54.
> Lingard, i. 161-163.
> Wheeler, 44-51.

Danish Invasions,

> Allen, 125-141.
> Armitage, 46-50.
> Bright, i. 7.
> Church, 202-205.
> Dickens, 17.
> Freeman, Sh. Hist. Nor. Conq., 8.
> Freeman, Old Eng. Hist., 108-113, 117-123.
> Gardiner, i. 57, 58.
> Green, Eng. Peo., i. 73-75.
> Green, Sh. Hist., 45-47.
> Green, Conquest, 96-105.
> Hughes, 68-113.
> Hume, 43-45.
> Knight, i. 93-104.
> Lappenberg, ii. 60-73.
> Lingard, i. 163-171.
> Thierry, i. 67, 68.

English Conquest

Guthrum,
Treaty of Wedmore,
{ Allen, 137, 138.
Armitage, 51.
Bright, i. 7. 8.
Church, 206-208.
Dickens, 18.
Freeman, i. 31, 32, 37.
Freeman, Old Eng. Hist., 123-127.
Gardiner, i. 58-60.
Green, Eng. Peo., i. 74, 75.
Green, Sh. Hist., 47-50.
Green, Conquest, 107.
Hughes, 105-113, 127.
Hume, 44, 45.
Johnson, 19-21.
Knight, i. 105-107.
Lappenberg, ii. 65.
Lingard, i. 172-174.
Thierry, i. 69, 70. }

Improvements,
Strongholds,
Palaces, Navy,
Army, Laws,
{ Allen, 138, 139.
Armitage, 52, 53, 60.
Church, 215-219.
Freeman, i. 35-37.
Freeman, Old Eng. Hist., 132, 133.
Gardiner, i. 60, 61.
Green, Conquest, 127-140.
Green, Eng. Peo., i. 81.
Hughes, 44, 45, 139-141, 149-153, 160-167.
Knight, i. 108, 109.
Lappenberg, ii. 77-82.
Lingard, i. 174-181. }

Literary Work,
{ Allen, 139.
Armitage, 53-56.
Church, 219-224.
Dickens, 19.
Freeman, Old Eng. Hist., 130, 131.
Gardiner, i. 60-62.
Green, Eng. Peo., i. 78-80.
Green, Sh. Hist., 51, 52.
Green, Conquest, 149-161.
Hughes, 278-300.
Hume, 46. }

English History

Literary Work,
(Continued.)
- Knight, i. 110-112.
- Lappenberg, ii. 82-85.
- Lingard, i. 179, 180.

Hastings,
- Allen, 138.
- Armitage, 58, 59.
- Bright, i. 9.
- Church, 209-214.
- Dickens, 18.
- Freeman, Old Eng. Hist., 136, 137.
- Green, Eng. Peo., i. 81.
- Green, Sh. Hist., 53.
- Green, Conquest, 162-167.
- Hughes, 251-263.
- Knight, i. 114-116.
- Lappenberg, ii. 66, 67.
- Lingard, i. 182-187.

Character,
- Allen, 136, 137.
- Armitage, 61.
- Bright, i. 9.
- Dickens, 20, 21.
- Freeman, i. 33-36, 48-52.
- Freeman, Old Eng. Hist., 113, 114.
- Green, Eng. Peo., i. 75-79.
- Green, Sh. Hist., 50, 51.
- Green, Conquest, 167-169, 178-180.
- Hughes, 307-309.
- Hume, 45, 46.
- Knight, i. 115, 116.
- Lappenberg, ii. 100-102.
- Thierry, i. 66, 67.

Dunstan,
Six Boy Kings,
- Allen, 141-150, 164-169.
- Armitage, 64-73.
- Bright, i. 10-19.
- Church, 232-264.
- Dickens, 22-30.
- Freeman, i. 37-46, 177-181, 225-228, 254-257.
- Freeman, Old Eng. Hist., 138-233.
- Gardiner, i. 63-69.
- Green, Eng. Peo., i. 82-86, 95-99.
- Green, Sh. Hist., 54-62.

English Conquest   17

Dunstan,
Six Boy Kings,
(Continued.)

{ Hume, 49-55.
Jewett, 171-173.
Knight, i. 121-138, 142-149, 155.
Lingard, i. 207-254. }

— DANISH LINE.

Sweyn, Canute,
Harold,
Hardicanute,

{ Allen, 169, 170.
Armitage, 73-88.
Bright, i. 20, 21.
Church, 262, 276, 277, 285-319.
Dickens, 30-37.
Freeman, i. 247, 266-273, 290-293, 320-326.
Freeman, Old Eng. Hist., 211-251.
Freeman, Sh. Hist. Nor. Conq., 13-15, 17-24.
Gardiner, i. 79-86.
Green, Eng. Peo., i. 98-103.
Green, Sh. Hist., 64-67.
Green, Conquest of Eng., 392-409.
Hume, 57-61.
Jewett, 178-184.
Knight, i. 156-161.
Lappenberg, ii. 240-248, 265-270, 277-284.
Lingard, i. 237-277.
Wheeler, 57-61. }

ENGLISH LINE.

Godwin,

{ Allen, 170.
Armitage, 89-95.
Bright, i. 20-23.
Church, 328-335.
Dickens, 37-40.
Freeman, Sh. Hist. Conq., 25, 26, 28, 39-41.
Freeman, i. 274, 275, 283, 285, ii. 20-22, 84-104, 232-235.
Freeman, Old Eng. Hist., 259-262, 264-269.
Gardiner, i. 86-89.
Green, Eng. Peo., i. 103-105.
Green, Sh. Hist., 67-70.
Green, Conq., 460-465, 480-483, 508-510, 514-521. }

English History

Godwin,
(Continued.)

- Hume, 62-64.
- Hunt, 64-68.
- Jewett, 184, 188, 189.
- Knight, i. 162-167, 171.
- Lappenberg, ii. 286, 287, 300-304, 313-315.
- Lingard, i. 279, 282, 285-292.
- Thierry, i. 114-118, 122, 123, 128-132, 136-140.
- Yonge, i. 23-29.

Edward the Confessor,

- Allen, 170.
- Armitage, 88.
- Bright, i. 21-24.
- Church, 320-323.
- Dickens, 43-49.
- Freeman, Sh. Hist. Nor. Conq., 24, 25.
- Freeman, i. 354, ii. 3-11, 14-18, 337-343.
- Freeman, Old Eng. Hist., 252, 253, 258-262, 269, 270, 293-296.
- Gardiner, i. 86-89.
- Green, Eng. Peo., i. 103-106.
- Green, Sh. Hist., 68-70.
- Green, Conquest, 467, 468, 472, 473.
- Hume, 61-66.
- Jewett, 186-194.
- Johnson, 109-116.
- Knight, i. 162-167, 176.
- Lappenberg, ii. 285-291, 296-300, 332.
- Lingard, i. 277-285, 303-306.
- Thierry, i. 124-127.
- Yonge, i. 26-29.

Harold,

- Armitage, 95-104.
- Bright, i. 23-27.
- Church, 340-343, 351-360.
- Dickens, 37-42.
- Freeman, Sh. Hist. Nor. Conq., 43-63.
- Freeman, ii. 23-28, 236-240, 244-246, 261, 270, 271, 283.
- Freeman, Old Eng. Hist., 297-348.
- Gardiner, i. 89-98.
- Green, Eng. Peo., i. 106, 107, 111, 112.
- Green, Sh. Hist., 70.

Harold.
(*Continued.*)

{ Green, Conquest, 535, 545-548.
Hume, 66-69.
Hunt, 68-75.
Jewett, 255-272.
Johnson, 125-131.
Knight, i. 172-177, 181-183.
Lappenberg, ii. 327-329, 334, 335.
Lingard, i. 300-303, 306-319.
Thierry, i. 141-143, 146-157.
Yonge, i. 30-37.

COWPER: *Cædwalla, or Saxons in Isle of Wight.*
BULWER: *Harold, the Last of the Saxon Kings.*
HENTY: *The Dragon and the Raven.*
KINGSLEY: *Hereward, the Last of the English.*
SCOTT: *Harold the Dauntless.*
TENNYSON: *Harold.*
SHAKESPEARE: *Macbeth.*

Norman Conquest. 1066-1154.

William the Conqueror. 1066-1087.

Montgomery, 58-70.   Anderson, 72-81, 84-92.   Towle, 54-71.

In Normandy,
- Allen, 170-173.
- Armitage, 104, 105.
- Bright, i. 24-26.
- Church, 344, 350, 361-369.
- Freeman, Sh. Hist. Nor. Conq., 30-38.
- Freeman, William the Conq., 34-50.
- Freeman, ii. 110, 113-124, iv. 64, 65.
- Freeman, Old Eng. Hist., 262, 263.
- Gardiner, i. 88, 89.
- Green, Eng. Peo., i. 109-112.
- Green, Sh. Hist., 76-78.
- Green, Conquest, 457, 472, 499-502.
- Hume, 79-81.
- Hunt, 34-44.
- Jewett, 166-170, 195-216.
- Johnson, 86-91, 116-125.
- Knight, i. 177.
- Lingard, ii. 2, 3.
- Thierry, i. 134, 135, 159-165.
- Yonge, i. 18-22.

Senlac, 1066.
- Armitage, 104-109.
- Bright, i. 26, 27.
- Church, 369-375.
- Creasy, 182-214.
- Dickens, 45-47.
- Freeman, William the Conq., 82-91.
- Freeman, iii. 266-273, 301-344.
- Freeman, Sh. Hist. of Nor. Conq., 71-85.
- Gardiner, i. 96-98.
- Green, Eng. Peo., i. 113-115.

Senlac, 1066,
(Continued.)

Green, Sh. Hist., 78-80.
Green, Conquest, 549-551.
Hume, 68, 69.
Hunt, 77-80.
Jewett, 304-311.
Johnson, 131-135.
Knight, i. 180-182.
Lappenberg, ii. 355-370.
Lingard, i. 311-319.
Thierry, i. 165-179.
Wheeler, 67-71.
Yonge, i. 43-49.

Crowning of William,

Armitage, 111.
Bright, i. 41, 42.
Dickens, 48, 49.
Freeman, Nor. Conq., iii. 373-375.
Freeman, Sh. Hist. Conq., 87-89.
Freeman, William the Conq., 94-97.
Gardiner, i. 98-100.
Green, Eng. Peo., i. 115.
Green, Sh. Hist., 81.
Green, Conquest, 551, 552.
Hume, 82, 83.
Jewett, 314.
Knight, i. 185, 186.
Lingard, ii. 6, 7.
Thierry, i. 188, 189.

Resistance of England,

Armitage, 111-115.
Bright, i. 40-42, 45-47, 50, 51.
Dickens, 49-52.
Freeman, Nor. Conq., iv. 3-5.
Freeman, Sh. Hist., 93-108.
Freeman, William the Conq., 93-96, 110-121, 150-156.
Gardiner, i. 101-104.
Green, Eng. Peo., i. 116-118.
Green, Sh. Hist., 82, 83.
Green, Conq. of England, 553-556.
Hume, 84-87.
Hunt, 82-89.

English History

Resistance of England,
(Continued.)

Jewett, 315, 316, 325-331.
Johnson, 154-158.
Knight, i. 186-190, 192-199.
Lingard, ii. 3, 4, 7, 11-38.
Thierry, i. 200-208, 212-227, 239-243, 263-272.
Yonge, i. 50-57.

Feudalism,
a. **In England,**
b. **Under William,**

Armitage, 77-88, 117-122.
Bright, i. 28-37.
Freeman, Nor. Conq., i. 62, 63, iii. 87-90, v. 42, 246-325.
Freeman, Sh. Hist., 125, 126.
Freeman, William the Conq., 121-136.
Gardiner, i. 104, 105, 113.
Green, Eng. Peo., i. 92-94, 127-131.
Green, Sh. Hist., 83-85.
Hume, 71, 72, 124, 125.
Hunt, 2, 3, 5, 90-92, 99-101, 115-121, 153.
Jewett, 316-319.
Johnson, 140-154, 158-161.
Knight, i. 214, 215.
Lingard, i. 320-337, ii. 45-52.

Domesday Book,
New Forest,
Curfew,
Tower of London,
Churches,
Castles,

Armitage, 122, 123.
Bright, i. 38, 39, 43, 55.
Dickens, 53.
Freeman, William the Conq., 171, 189, 191.
Freeman, Nor. Conq., ii. 113, iii. 370, 371, iv. 43, 44, 107, 145, 412-414, 469-472, v. 1-3, 432-434.
Freeman, Sh. Hist., 124, 125.
Gardiner, i. 104, 110-112.
Green, Sh. Hist., 85-87.
Hume, 91-93.
Hunt, 85, 92-98, 134-136.
Jewett, 251, 331.
Johnson, 178.
Knight, i. 203-206, 211, 213.
Lingard, ii. 56, 57.
Thierry, i. 196, 301-304.
Yonge, i. 65-67.

Norman Conquest

Character of William,
- Armitage, 110, 124, 125.
- Freeman, Nor. Conq., ii. 107-113, 136. iii. 53, 108, 109, 180, iv. 418-425, 436.
- Freeman, Sh. Hist., 140.
- Freeman, William the Conq. 195-200.
- Green, Eng. Peo., i. 125, 126.
- Green, Sh. Hist., 74-76.
- Hume, 92.
- Hunt, 130-133.
- Jewett, 149-151, 342-344.
- Johnson, 86.
- Knight, i. 191, 218, 219.
- Lingard, ii. 68-71.
- Wheeler, 72-77.
- Yonge, i. 64, 65.

Character and Results of Conquest.
- Armitage, 115-121, 130-133.
- Bright, i. 36, 37, 42, 43.
- Freeman, Nor. Conq., ii. 226, iv. 8, v. 42, 43, 226-228, 262-265.
- Freeman, Sh. Hist., 1-5, 136-147.
- Green, Conq., 520, 521.
- Green, Eng. Peo., i. 130-132, 135, 136.
- Johnson, 221-238.
- Stubbs, 11, 12.

WILLIAM RUFUS. 1087-1100.

Montgomery, 70-72. Anderson, 81. Towle, 72-76.

Character of Reign,
- Armitage, 134-139.
- Bright, i. 56-62.
- Dickens, 56-62.
- Freeman, Nor. Conq., v. 47-50, 97, 98.
- Gardiner, i. 114-121.
- Green, Eng. Peo., i. 136-140.
- Green, Sh. Hist., 89, 90.
- Hume, 95-98.
- Hunt, 138-144, 169.
- Jewett, 345-353.
- Johnson, 182-192, 197-200.
- Knight, i. 219-231.
- Lingard, ii. 15-103.
- Wheeler, 77-82.
- Yonge, i. 77-84.

24   *English History*

First Crusade, 1096.
{ Armitage. 201-210.
Dickens. 59-61.
Freeman, Nor. Conq., v. 60-63.
Gardiner, i. 120. 121.
Hume, 96, 97.
Jewett, 351. 352.
Johnson, 192-197.
Knight, i. 226-230.
Lingard, ii. 83-85.
Yonge, i. 86-94. }

HENRY I. 1100–1135.

Montgomery, 73-75.   Anderson, 81-84.   Towle, 77-82.

**Charter,
Marriage,**
{ Armitage, 145.
Bright, i. 63, 64, 73-76.
Dickens. 63. 64.
Freeman, v. 110-112.
Gardiner, i. 123, 124.
Green, Eng. Peo., i. 140-142.
Green. Sh. Hist., 91.
Hume, 99.
Hunt, 186-188.
Jewett, 354.
Johnson. 202. 203.
Knight. i. 233-237.
Lingard, ii. 105-109.
Thierry, i. 343-349. }

**Quarrel with
Robert,**
{ Bright, 65, 66.
Dickens, 64-67.
Freeman, Nor. Conq., v. 114-118.
Gardiner, i. 124, 125.
Green, Eng. Peo., i. 141-143.
Hume, 99-101.
Johnson. 203. 204.
Knight. i. 233-241.
Lingard, ii. 109-115, 119, 120, 144.
Yonge, i. 102-105. }

Angevin Marriage,
- Armitage, 149.
- Bright, i. 67-69.
- Dickens, 68.
- Freeman, Nor. Conq., v. 132-138.
- Gardiner, i. 131.
- Green, Eng. Peo., i. 146, 147, 150.
- Green, Sh. Hist., 100, 101.
- Hume, 101, 102.
- Johnson, 213.
- Knight, i. 244, 245.
- Lingard, ii. 120, 129-133.
- Yonge, i. 121, 122.

Administration.
- Armitage, 146-149.
- Bright, i. 74-76.
- Freeman, v. 102-110.
- Gardiner, i. 126, 127.
- Green, Eng. Peo., i. 143-146.
- Green, Sh. Hist., 96, 97.
- Hunt, 190-197.
- Johnson, 216, 221.
- Lingard, ii. 133-141.
- Wheeler, 82-85.

STEPHEN. 1135-1154.

Montgomery, 75-77.   Anderson, 84-86.   Towle, 83, 84.

Battle of the Standard, Civil War.
- Armitage, 149-152.
- Bright, i. 80-88.
- Dickens, 73-76.
- Freeman, v. 162-170, 176-178, 189, 190, 195-210.
- Gardiner, i. 131-137.
- Green, Eng. Peo., i. 151-160.
- Green, Sh. Hist., 101-104.
- Hume, 103-106.
- Hunt, 198-209.
- Knight, i. 249-253, 261-269.
- Lingard, ii. 156-187.
- Stubbs, 14-34.
- Thierry, ii. 25-32.
- Yonge, i. 125-134.

The Angevins or Plantagenets. 1154-1399.

Henry II. 1154-1189.

Montgomery, 87-97. Anderson, 95-102. Towle, 84-99.

Thomas à Becket, Chancellor, Archbishop,
- Armitage, 161-168.
- Bright, i. 92, 95.
- Dickens, 77-85.
- Freeman, Nor. Conq., v. 441-443.
- Gardiner, i. 140-143.
- Green, Eng. Peo., i. 163-165.
- Green, Sh. Hist., 106.
- Mrs. Green, 24-26, 78-81, 86-104.
- Hume, 109-112.
- Knight, i. 271-273, 280-283.
- Lingard, ii. 197-206.
- Stubbs, 67-74.
- Thierry, ii. 52-61.
- Yonge, i. 135-141.

Constitutions of Clarendon, Assize of Clarendon, and other Reforms,
- Armitage, 152-158, 168-172, 181-183, 186, 187.
- Bright, i. 93-97, 106-109, 113, 114.
- Dickens, 82, 83.
- Freeman, v. 449-457.
- Gardiner, i. 143-148, 154, 155.
- Green, Eng. Peo., i. 162-168, 179, 180.
- Green, Sh. Hist., 106-112.
- Mrs. Green, 68-126.
- Hume, 111, 118.
- Knight, i. 283, 287, 301, 302.
- Lingard, ii. 213-220, 283-298, 310, 311.
- Stubbs, 39-48, 55-58, 76, 77, 85-88.
- Thierry, ii. 65-71.
- Yonge, i. 142-148.

The Angevins or Plantagenets 27

Condemnation, Exile, and Death of Becket,
- Armitage, 170-179.
- Bright, i. 98-101.
- Dickens, 85-88.
- Freeman, v. 443-447.
- Gardiner, i. 143-151.
- Green, Eng. Peo., i. 166, 168-170.
- Green, Sh. Hist., 108, 109.
- Mrs. Green, 104-115, 133-135, 148-152.
- Hume, 112-115.
- Knight, i. 290-293.
- Lingard, ii. 221-227, 230-245.
- Stubbs, 74-84.
- Thierry, ii. 71-86, 101-111.
- Wheeler, 87-92.
- Yonge, i. 146-156.

Ireland,
- Armitage, 196-200.
- Bright, i. 102, 103.
- Dickens, 88-90.
- Gardiner, i. 151, 152.
- Green, Eng. Peo., i. 175-177.
- Green, Sh. Hist., 112.
- Mrs. Green, 155-169.
- Hume, 115-117.
- Knight, i. 296-299.
- Lingard, ii. 260-265.
- Stubbs, 91.
- Thierry, ii. 125, 127-135.
- Towle, Ireland, 49-71.
- Yonge, i. 159-169.

Civil War,
- Armitage, 183-185.
- Bright, i. 103-105.
- Gardiner, i. 153-157.
- Green, Sh. Hist., 109.
- Mrs. Green, 170-190.
- Hume, 117, 118.
- Knight, i. 299-301.
- Lingard, ii. 271-282.
- Stubbs, 95-98.

Character,
- Armitage, 187-189.
- Gardiner, i. 138, 157, 158.

English History

Character.
(Continued.)

- Green, Eng. Peo., i. 161, 162.
- Green, Sh. Hist., 103-105.
- Mrs. Green, 1, 2, 11-20.
- Hume, 119, 120.
- Knight, i. 274, 275.
- Lingard, ii. 194-196.
- Stubbs, 36-39.

RICHARD I. 1189-1199.

Montgomery, 97-103.   Anderson, 102-106.   Towle, 100-102.

Zeal against Infidels.

- Bright, i. 115-123.
- Dickens, 96-104.
- Freeman, Nor. Conq., v. 459-466.
- Gardiner, i. 159-165.
- Green, Eng. Peo., i. 183-188.
- Green, Sh. Hist., 112-114.
- Hume, 120.
- Knight, i. 305-320.
- Lingard, ii. 314-356.
- Stubbs, 110-122, 128-130.
- Yonge, i. 181-193.

JOHN. 1199-1216.

Montgomery, 103-109.   Anderson, 106-111.   Towle, 102-111.

Loss of Normandy,

- Bright, i. 126-129.
- Dickens, 105-109.
- Freeman, Nor. Conq., v. 468-470.
- Gardiner, i. 173-176.
- Green, Eng. Peo., i. 189, 190.
- Green, Sh. Hist., 115.
- Hume, 132, 133.
- Knight, i. 333-336.
- Lingard, iii. 4-14.
- Stubbs, 140-144.
- Yonge, i. 201-205.

The Angevins or Plantagenets

Contest with Church, Stephen Langton,
- Bright, i. 130-136.
- Dickens, 109-112.
- Freeman, Nor. Conq., v. 472, 473.
- Gardiner, i. 176-180.
- Green, Eng. Peo., i. 229-239.
- Hume, 134-137.
- Knight, i. 337-343.
- Lingard, iii. 15-45.
- Stubbs, 147-150.
- Yonge, i. 206-214.

Magna Charta, 1215.
- Bright, i. 137-139.
- Dickens, 112-116.
- Freeman, Nor. Conq., v. 474-479.
- Gardiner, i. 180-184.
- Green, Eng. Peo., i. 240-249.
- Green, Sh. Hist., 128-132.
- Hume, 137-140.
- Knight, i. 345-351.
- Lingard, iii. 45-72.
- Stubbs, 151-158.
- Wheeler, 96-100.
- Yonge, i. 215-221.

HENRY III. 1216–1272.

Montgomery, 103-115. Anderson, 111-114. Towle, 112-118.

Simon de Montford, Mad Parliament,
- Bright, i. 152-161.
- Dickens, 124-128.
- Gardiner, i. 192-200.
- Green, Eng. Peo., i. 274-278, 290-295.
- Green, Sh. Hist., 152-156.
- Hume, 145, 146.
- Knight, i. 371-373.
- Lingard, iii. 118-127.
- Stubbs, 193-199.
- Yonge, i. 250-257.

Barons' Wars, Lewes, Evesham,
- Bright, i. 162-168.
- Dickens, 124-128.
- Green, Eng. Peo., i. 295-304.
- Green, Sh. Hist., 157-160.

English History

**Barons' Wars,
Lewes,
Evesham,**
(*Continued.*)

- Hume, 147-148.
- Knight, i. 373-376.
- Stubbs, 200-209.
- Wheeler, 116-121.
- Yonge, i. 258-263.

**House of Commons,
1265.**

- Bright, i. 164, 165.
- Gardiner, i. 199-203.
- Green, Eng. Peo., i. 299-301.
- Hume, 147, 148.
- Knight, i. 375, 376.
- Lingard, iii. 161-173.
- Stubbs, 207, 208.

EDWARD I. 1272-1307.

Montgomery, 115-121. Anderson, 114-121. Towle, 119-126.

Welsh Campaign,

- Bright, i. 175-177.
- Dickens, 132-135.
- Gardiner, i. 210.
- Green, Eng. Peo., i. 324, 325, 332-334.
- Green, Sh. Hist., 161-169.
- Hume, 153, 154.
- Knight, i. 383, 384, 387-390.
- Lingard, iii. 188-198, 218.
- Stubbs, 217-220.

**Banishment of
Jews,**

- Bright, i. 179.
- Dickens, 131, 132.
- Green, Eng. Peo., i. 336-341.
- Green, Sh. Hist., 205.
- Hume, 155.
- Knight, i. 386, 387.
- Lingard, iii. 248-254.
- Stubbs, 239, 240.
- Yonge, i. 282, 283.

**Trouble with
France,**

- Bright, i. 184-190.
- Dickens, 135-137.
- Gardiner, i. 216-218.
- Hume, 157, 158, 160.
- Lingard, iii. 214-218.
- Stubbs, 243, 244.
- Yonge, i. 299-303.

The Angevins or Plantagenets 31

Scotland,
William Wallace,
Robert Bruce,

- Bright, i. 180-186, 189-192.
- Dickens, 137-145.
- Gardiner, i. 215-224.
- Green, Eng. Peo., i. 341-346, 360-362, 365-371, 380, 381.
- Green, Sh. Hist., 187-193.
- Hume, 155-158, 160-162.
- Knight, i. 411-426.
- Lingard, iii. 200-245, 274-281.
- Stubbs, 240-243, 257-261.
- Wheeler, 121-125.
- Yonge, i. 288-298, 306-314.

Reforms in Church and State,
Model Parliament, 1295,

- Bright, i. 172-175, 185-188, 193-196.
- Gardiner, i. 212-214, 220, 221.
- Green, Eng. Peo., i. 321, 325-332, 334-336, 349-359, 362-365.
- Hume, 152, 157-159.
- Knight, i. 385, 386.
- Lingard, iii. 245-248, 263-274.
- Stubbs, 222-238, 248-256.
- Yonge, i. 281-285, 301-305.

Character.

- Bright, i. 172, 173.
- Gardiner, i. 208-210.
- Green, Eng. Peo., i. 313-321.
- Green, Sh. Hist., 181-184.
- Hume, 162.
- Stubbs, 212-215.
- Yonge, i. 280, 281.

EDWARD II. 1307–1327.

Montgomery, 121-124. Anderson, 122-126. Towle, 127-132.

Piers Gaveston,

- Bright, i. 197-206.
- Dickens, 146-149.
- Gardiner, i. 224-226.
- Green, Eng. Peo., i. 380-385.
- Green, Sh. Hist., 207-209.
- Hume, 162-164.
- Knight, i. 428-430.
- Lingard, iii. 283-296.

32   *English History*

| Piers Gaveston, (*Continued.*) | Stubbs, 263-273. Yonge, i. 315-322. |

Scotland Regains its Independence, 1314,
- Bright, i. 200-205.
- Dickens, 149, 150.
- Gardiner, i. 226-228.
- Green, Eng. Peo.. i. 385-389.
- Green, Sh. Hist., 209.
- Hume, 164, 165.
- Knight, i. 430-439.
- Lingard, iii. 298-302, 313-320.
- Stubbs, 266, 273-276, 282.
- Wheeler, 126-134.
- Yonge, i. 323-332.

New Favorites, Deposition of Edward.
- Bright, i. 205-211.
- Dickens, 150-155.
- Gardiner, i. 228-231.
- Green, Eng. Peo.. i. 389-392.
- Green, Sh. Hist., 209.
- Hume, 164-166.
- Knight, i. 441-443.
- Lingard, iii. 320-347.
- Stubbs, 277-290.
- Yonge, i. 340-351.

EDWARD III. 1327-1377.

Montgomery, 124-134.   Anderson, 126-133.   Towle, 133-140.

War with Scotland, Neville's Cross,
- Bright, i. 214-218, 228.
- Dickens, 158.
- Gardiner, i. 231-234, 242, 243.
- Green, Eng. Peo.. i. 399-402, 436, 437.
- Green, Sh. Hist., 223, 224, 228
- Hume, 169, 170, 175.
- Knight, i. 443-445, 451, 464.
- Lingard, iv. 1-7, 15-21, 77-81.
- Warburton, 8-16, 25-34, 90-92, 122-125, 160, 161.
- Yonge, ii. 26-32, 34-37, 57, 58.

The Angevins or Plantagenets

Rise of English Commerce, Causes of French War,
- Bright, i. 217-224.
- Dickens, 158, 159.
- Gardiner, i. 232-239.
- Green, Eng. Peo., i. 398, 399, 402-415.
- Green, Sh. Hist., 224, 225.
- Hume, 170-172.
- Knight, i. 452-454.
- Lingard, iv. 21-30.
- Warburton, 34-44, 55-78.
- Yonge, ii. 1-11.

Sluys, Crécy, Calais,
- Bright, i. 220, 224-228.
- Dickens, 160-163.
- Gardiner, i. 239-243.
- Green, Eng. Peo., i. 416-425.
- Green, Sh. Hist., 225-228.
- Hume, 173-176.
- Knight, i. 453, 456-467.
- Lingard, iv. 30-62.
- Warburton, 80-84, 107-133.
- Wheeler, 134-139.
- Yonge, ii. 38-53.

Black Death, Its Effects,
- Bright, i. 229.
- Dickens, 163.
- Gardiner, i. 246-250.
- Green, Eng. Peo., i. 428-433.
- Hume, 176.
- Knight, i. 469-472.
- Lingard, iv. 62-67.
- Warburton, 140-155.
- Wheeler, 140-144.
- Yonge, ii. 55, 56.

Poictiers, Treaty of Bretigny,
- Bright, i. 229-234.
- Dickens, 163-166.
- Gardiner, i. 251-254.
- Green, Eng. Peo., i. 434-438.
- Green, Sh. Hist., 229, 230.
- Hume, 177-180.
- Knight, i. 473-478, 483.
- Lingard, iv. 68-88.
- Warburton, 165-177, 190-192.
- Yonge, ii. 58-66.

34 *English History*

Black Prince in Castile,
Loss of French Possessions,
{ Bright, i. 234-236.
Dickens, 166, 167.
Gardiner, i. 254-257.
Green, Eng. Peo., i. 448-454.
Hume, 180, 181.
Knight, i. 483-487.
Lingard, iv. 89-100.
Warburton, 197-205, 217-232.
Yonge, ii. 88-109. }

Good Parliament,
{ Bright, i. 237-240.
Gairdner, 3.
Gardiner, i. 243-246, 262.
Green, Eng. Peo., i. 465, 466.
Green, Sh. Hist., 231-235.
Hume, 182, 226-228.
Lingard, iv. 101-105.
Warburton, 239-241. }

Character of King and Reign.
{ Green, Eng. Peo., i. 426-428, 438-440, 469, 470.
Green, Sh. Hist., 218, 219.
Hume, 181, 182.
Lingard, iv. 105-156.
Warburton, 256-263. }

, RICHARD II. 1377–1399.

Montgomery, 134-141. Anderson, 134-142. Towle, 141-154.

New Tax,
Wat Tyler,
{ Bright, i. 242-245.
Dickens, 169-173.
Gairdner, 12-19.
Gardiner, i. 267-269.
Green, Eng. Peo., i. 472-485.
Green, Sh. Hist., 251-253.
Hume, 184-186.
Knight, ii. 3-7.
Lingard, iv. 162-185.
Yonge, ii. 129-134. }

The Angevins or Plantagenets 35

Deposition,
- Bright, i. 248-254.
- Dickens, 173-177.
- Gairdner, 50-61.
- Gardiner, i. 278-285.
- Green, Eng. Peo., i. 517-521.
- Green, Sh. Hist., 264.
- Hume, 188, 189.
- Knight, ii. 23-38.
- Lingard, iv. 245-269.
- Wheeler, 149-154.
- Yonge, ii. 195-209.

Literature:

State of Language,
- Bright, i. 270-272.
- Gairdner, 62, 66, 67.
- Gardiner, i. 258.
- Green, Eng. Peo., i. 502, 503.
- Green, Sh. Hist., 217-219.
- Warburton, 257, 258, 274-277.
- Welsh, i. 173-176.

Wycliffe, Lollards,
- Bright, i. 266, 267.
- Froude, ii. 25-36.
- Gairdner, 4-8, 65.
- Gardiner, i. 261-263, 266.
- Green, Eng. Peo., i. 444-447, 467-469, 488-496.
- Green, Sh. Hist., 235-244.
- Hume, 190, 191.
- Knight, ii. 8-11.
- Lingard, iv. 157-161, 185-196, 233, 234.
- Warburton, 247-255.
- Wheeler, 144-149.
- Yonge, ii. 112-115, 118, 124, 142-144.

Chaucer,
- Bright, i. 273, 274.
- Gairdner, 63, 64.
- Gardiner, i. 270-272.
- Green, Eng. Peo., i. 504-509.
- Green, Sh. Hist., 219-223.
- Knight, i. 479-483, ii. 11, 12.
- Warburton, 279-281.
- Welsh, i. 204-232.
- Yonge, ii. 83, 113, 115, 135, 146, 180.

Wm. Langland.
{ Bright, i. 273.
  Gardiner, i. 258, 259, 266.
  Green, Eng. Peo., i. 440-443.
  Green, Sh. Hist., 255-257.
  Warburton. 278, 279.
  Welsh, i. 177-180.

DOYLE: *The White Company.*
EDGAR: *Great Men and Great Deeds* (Crusades).
FROISSART: *Chronicles.*
GILLIAT: *John Standish.*
HENTY: *Brothers in Arms, A Story of the Crusades; For the Temple, A Tale of the Fall of Jerusalem; In Freedom's Cause* (Wallace and Bruce); *St. George for England* (Crécy and Poictiers).
JAMES: *Forest Days* (Simon de Montford).
PORTER: *Scottish Chiefs.*
SCOTT: *Count Robert of Paris* (1090); *Betrothed* (1187); *Talisman* (1193); *Ivanhoe* (1194); *Castle Dangerous* (1306).
YONGE: *Prince and Page; The Constable's Tower.*
SHAKESPEARE: *King John; Edward III.; Richard II.*
GRAY: *The Bard* (1282).
SCOTT: *Lord of the Isles* (1307); *Halidon Hill* (1333).
SOUTHEY: *Wat Tyler. Chevy Chase.*

HOUSES OF LANCASTER AND YORK. 1399–1485.

HOUSE OF LANCASTER. 1399–1461.

HENRY IV. 1399–1413.

Montgomery, 150-154.   Anderson, 146-148.   Towle, 155-158.

Conspiracies and Revolts,
- Bright, i. 276-282.
- Church, 10-21.
- Dickens, 177-185.
- Gairdner, 67-72, 76-85.
- Gardiner, i. 285-298.
- Green, Eng. Peo., i. 524-533.
- Green, Sh. Hist., 265, 266.
- Hume, 193-195.
- Knight, ii. 40-50.
- Lingard, iv. 270, 271, 274-328.
- Yonge, ii. 209-236.

Persecution of Lollards.
- Bright, i. 284-286.
- Dickens, 180.
- Gairdner, 86-88.
- Gardiner, i. 291, 292.
- Green, Eng. Peo., i. 522-524, 533-536.
- Green, Sh. Hist., 265-267.
- Knight, ii. 44-46.
- Lingard, iv. 328-335.
- Yonge, ii. 236-242.

HENRY V. 1413–1422.

Montgomery, 155-158.   Anderson, 148-151.   Towle, 158-161.

Persecution of Lollards, Sir John Oldcastle,
- Bright, i. 287-289.
- Church, 97-104.
- Dickens, 186, 187.
- Gairdner, 93-96, 107, 108.
- Gardiner, i. 299, 300.

English History

Persecution of Lollards, Sir John Oldcastle, *(Continued.)*
- Green, Eng. Peo., i. 538-540.
- Green, Sh. Hist., 266, 267.
- Hume, 197.
- Knight, ii. 53-55.
- Lingard, v. 1-6, 31, 32.
- Yonge, ii. 242-246.

War with France:

Harfleur, Agincourt,
- Bright, i. 291-296.
- Church, 61-64, 67-91.
- Dickens, 187-192.
- Gairdner, 96-103.
- Gardiner, i. 300-303.
- Green, Eng. Peo., i. 540-543.
- Green, Sh. Hist., 267, 268.
- Hume, 197-199.
- Knight, ii. 55-64.
- Lingard, v. 6-30.
- Wheeler, 154-160.
- Yonge, ii. 266-284.

Siege of Rouen, Treaty of Troyes.
- Bright, i. 298-301.
- Church, 109-130.
- Dickens, 193-195.
- Gairdner, 107-113.
- Gardiner, i. 303-306.
- Green, Eng. Peo., i. 543-545.
- Green, Sh. Hist., 269-270.
- Hume, 199, 200.
- Knight, ii. 67-72.
- Lingard, v. 32-48.
- Yonge, ii. 296-305, 322-324.

HENRY VI. 1422–1461.

Montgomery, 158-164. Anderson, 151-157. Towle, 162-171.

Renewal of War:

Orleans, Joan of Arc,
- Bright, i. 304-311.
- Creasy, 218-236.
- Dickens, 196-205.
- Gairdner, 130-147.

Houses of Lancaster and York

**Orleans,
Joan of Arc,**
(Continued.)

- Gardiner, i. 307-313.
- Green, Eng. Peo., i. 546-559.
- Green, Sh. Hist., 274-279.
- Hume, 201-205.
- Knight, ii. 81-91.
- Lingard, v. 55-91.
- Wheeler, 161-166.
- Yonge, ii. 341, 342, 361-395.

Loss of French Possessions,

- Bright, i. 312-319.
- Dickens, 205-207.
- Gairdner, 148-161.
- Gardiner, i. 313-320.
- Green, Eng. Peo., i. 562, 563, 568, 569.
- Green, Sh. Hist., 279-281.
- Hume, 205-208.
- Knight, ii. 91-93.
- Lingard, v. 115-131, 143-145.
- Yonge, iii. 44-56.

Jack Cade's Rebellion,

- Bright, i. 319-321.
- Dickens, 208-210.
- Gairdner, 155-158.
- Gardiner, i. 320-323.
- Green, Eng. Peo., i. 564-568.
- Green, Sh. Hist., 281-283.
- Hume, 208, 209.
- Knight, ii. 131-135.
- Lingard, v. 133-143.
- Yonge, iii. 57-64.

Wars of Roses. 1455-1485.

First Battles.

- Bright, i. 320-327.
- Dickens, 210-214.
- Gairdner, 161-173.
- Gardiner, i. 323-329.
- Green, Eng. Peo., i. 570-576.
- Green, Sh. Hist., 283-285.
- Hume, 209-212.
- Knight, ii. 134-146.
- Lingard, v. 148-171.
- Yonge, iii. 95-114.

English History

HOUSE OF YORK. 1461-1485.

EDWARD IV. 1461-1483.

Montgomery, 167-169. Anderson, 157-160. Towle, 169-171, 177, 178.

Continuation of War,
- Bright, i. 328-340.
- Dickens, 214-222.
- Gairdner, 173-209.
- Gardiner, i. 329-336.
- Green, Eng. Peo., ii. 26, 27, 32, 39-47.
- Green, Sh. Hist., 285-288.
- Hume, 213-219.
- Knight, ii. 152-166.
- Lingard, v. 173-235.
- Yonge, iii. 114-116, 131-140.

Warwick, the King-maker,
- Bright, i. 322-327, 331-335.
- Dickens, 217-220.
- Gairdner, 163-168, 179-181, 183, 185-194.
- Gardiner, i. 331-334, 354.
- Green, Eng. Peo., ii. 24-45.
- Green, Sh. Hist., 286, 287.
- Hume, 207, 210, 211, 214-217.
- Knight, ii. 156-165.
- Yonge, iii. 127-140.

Introduction of Printing.
- Bright, i. 353.
- Gardiner, i. 358.
- Green, Eng. Peo., ii. 52-59.
- Green, Sh. Hist., 295, 296.
- Knight, ii. 200, 201.
- Lingard, v. 236-251.
- Yonge, iii. 83-85, 122, 165.

EDWARD V. 1483.

RICHARD III. 1483-1485.

Montgomery, 169-174. Anderson, 160-164. Towle, 172-179.

Revolts, Bosworth Field,
- Bright, i. 341-349.
- Dickens, 228-232.
- Gairdner, 209-236.

Revolts, Bosworth Field, (*Continued.*)	Gardiner, i. 337-343. Green, Eng. Peo., ii. 59-66. Green, Sh. Hist., 299-301. Hume, 222-224. Knight, ii. 193-207. Lingard, v. 252-271. Wheeler, 176-180. Yonge, iii. 174-192.
Effects of Wars.	Bright, i. 350-354. Gairdner, 236-239. Green, Eng. Peo., ii. 5-26. Green, Sh. Hist., 301. Hume, 225.

BULWER: *The Last of the Barons.*
FULLERTON: *A Stormy Life* (Warwick).
JAMES: *Agincourt.*
SCOTT: *Fair Maid of Perth* (1402).
YONGE: *The Caged Lion* (James of Scotland); *Two Penniless Princesses.*
SHAKESPEARE: *King Henry IV.; King Henry V.; King Henry VI.; Richard III.*
SCHILLER: *Maid of Orleans.*

THE TUDORS. 1485–1603.

HENRY VII. 1485–1509.

Montgomery, 179 187.   Anderson, 171-175   Towle, 180-183.

The Two Pretenders,
- Bright, ii. 358-362.
- Dickens, 233-241.
- Gairdner, Henry vii., 48-62. 102-120.
- Gardiner, i. 343-348, 350-352.
- Green, Eng. Peo., ii. 68, 69, 72, 73.
- Green, Sh. Hist., 301, 302.
- Hume, 231-236.
- Knight, ii. 212-214, 221-233.
- Lingard, v. 272-290, 304-324.
- Moberly, 27-34, 42-49.
- Towle, Ireland, 102-105.
- Yonge, iii. 193-201, 225-231.

Foreign Alliances, Star Chamber,
- Bright, ii. 359, 363-365.
- Dickens, 241.
- Gairdner, Henry vii., 164-183.
- Gardiner, i. 348-351.
- Green, Eng. Peo., ii. 74-77, 90, 91.
- Green, Sh. Hist., 302.
- Hume, 237-239.
- Knight, ii. 234-243.
- Lingard, v. 290-304.
- Moberly, 55-62, 71-73.
- Yonge, iii. 271-286.

Discoveries, New Learning.
- Dickens, 242, 243.
- Gardiner, ii. 352-356.
- Green, Eng. Peo., ii. 77-87, 93-105.
- Green, Sh. Hist., 303-307.
- Hume, 239.
- Knight, ii. 245-250.
- Lingard, v. 338-342.
- Moberly, 76-98.
- Yonge, iii. 272, 287-299.

The Tudors 43

HENRY VIII. 1509-1547.

Montgomery, 187-201. Anderson, 175-189. Towle, 183-196.

Battle of Spurs, Flodden,
- Bright, ii. 369-372.
- Creighton, Wolsey, 23-27.
- Dickens, 244-246.
- Gardiner, ii. 364, 405-409.
- Green, Eng. Peo., ii. 92, 93.
- Green, Sh. Hist., 311, 312, 380.
- Hume, 242, 243.
- Knight, ii. 263-272.
- Lingard, vi. 5-27.
- Moberly, 114-122.
- Yonge, iii. 310-338.

Wolsey's Rise and Greatness,
- Bright, ii. 375-380.
- Creighton, Wolsey, 18-149, 211-221.
- Dickens, 247, 248.
- Gardiner, ii. 363-366, 371-377.
- Green, Eng. Peo., ii. 106, 107, 110-113, 116-123.
- Green, Sh. Hist., 322-331.
- Hume, 242-244.
- Knight, ii. 264-268, 274-279.
- Lingard, vi. 33-44, 58-62.
- Moberly, 136-138.
- Yonge, iii. 282, 283, 362-366.

Austrian Alliance, Charles V.,
- Bright, ii. 378, 379.
- Creighton, Wolsey, 76-100.
- Dickens, 248-250.
- Gardiner, ii. 369-372.
- Green, Eng. Peo., ii. 108, 109, 113-123.
- Green, Sh. Hist., 324.
- Hume, 245-250.
- Knight, ii. 280-288.
- Lingard, vi. 45-63.
- Moberly, 138-143.
- Yonge, iii. 375-386.

44 English History

Divorce from Catherine,
Fall of Wolsey,

Bright, ii. 384-388.
Creighton, 150-210.
Dickens, 251-255.
Froude, i. 99-160, 193, 194, 238, 239, 272-278, 436-446.
Gardiner, ii. 379-384.
Green, Eng. Peo., ii. 133-141, 149, 150, 153.
Green, Sh. Hist., 329, 331.
Hume, 250-254, 257.
Knight, ii. 309-324.
Lingard, vi. 109-189.
Moberly, 156-167.
Wheeler, 185-190.
Yonge, iv. 29-40, 59, 60.

Act of Supremacy,
Subjection of Parliament,
Suppression of Monasteries and Results,
Separation of Church from Rome,

Bright, ii. 394-410.
Dickens, 258-263.
Froude, ii. 396-435, 322-324.
Gardiner, ii. 385, 396, 390-400.
Green, Eng. Peo., ii. 146, 147, 152-163, 171, 172, 197-204.
Green, Sh. Hist., 337-347.
Hume, 251-266.
Knight, ii. 355-358, 366-379, 397-414.
Lingard, vi. 201-218, 227-234, 253-268, 368-377.
Moberly, 167-171, 187-208.
Yonge, iv. 53-66, 86-98.

Thomas Cromwell,
Execution of More and Fisher,

Bright, ii. 389-396.
Dickens, 251, 256-258.
Froude, ii. 226-232, 359-376, iii. 405-410, 446-457, 474-480.
Gardiner, ii. 387, 388, 393, 394, 400, 401.
Green, Eng. Peo., ii. 141-145, 150-152, 164-173, 188-191.
Green, Sh. Hist., 332-348.
Hume, 256-266.
Knight, ii. 352-356, 362-368, 426-430.
Lingard, vi. 175-177, 209-224, 302-309.
Moberly, 171-187, 213-217.
Wheeler, 190-194.
Yonge, iv. 53-71, 76-82, 86-97.

The Tudors

Reformation:

Germany,
Martin Luther,

- Bright, ii. 383, 384.
- Dickens, 250.
- Froude, ii. 39, 40.
- Gardiner, ii. 377-379.
- Green, Eng. Peo., ii. 123-126.
- Hume, 247.
- Knight, ii. 289-291.
- Lingard, vi. 89-108.
- Moberly, 150-155.
- Yonge, iii. 342-356, 386-399.

England,
Tyndale,
Latimer,
Henry's Religious Changes.

- Bright, ii. 398, 410-412, 419-421.
- Froude, ii. 40-42, 333, 334, 359-376, iii. 80-87, 98-108.
- Gardiner, ii. 390, 396, 417.
- Green, Eng. Peo., ii. 126-131, 178-181, 186-191, 217-220.
- Green, Sh. Hist., 351-360, 366.
- Hume, 259, 265.
- Knight, ii. 338, 420-422.
- Lingard, vi. 268-284, 290-297, 317-319.
- Moberly, 155, 156, 192, 193, 236, 237, 242.
- Yonge, iv. 61.

EDWARD VI. 1547-1553.

Montgomery, 201-204.   Anderson, 189-194.   Towle, 196-201.

Cranmer,
Prayer Book,
Thirty-nine Articles,
Dissatisfaction,
Lady Jane Grey,

- Bright, ii. 442-447, 451.
- Creighton, Age of Eliz., 14-29.
- Dickens, 262-273.
- Froude, v. 43-49, 64, 140, 141, 170-207, vi. 19-33, 42, 43, 180, 184.
- Gardiner, ii. 412-420.
- Green, Eng. Peo., ii. 224-242.
- Green, Sh. Hist., 361, 362.
- Hume, 273-281, 286.
- Knight, iii. 9-13, 46-48, 51-56, 65-67.
- Lingard, vii. 17-122.
- Yonge, iv. 144-158, 166-190, 199, 200.

MARY. 1553-1558.

Montgomery, 204-208.   Anderson, 194-197.   Towle, 202-206.

Philip II.,
> Bright, ii. 448-455, 459-461.
> Creighton, 32-37, 87-90.
> Dickens, 277-280.
> Froude, vi. 70, 71, 102-109, 119-123, 132-140, 150, 151, 188, 190, 207, 222-229.
> Gardiner, ii. 421-423.
> Green, Eng. Peo., ii. 246-256.
> Green, Sh. Hist., 362, 363, 368, 369.
> Hume, 285-287.
> Knight, iii. 58-60, 74, 75.
> Lingard, vii. 137-186.
> Yonge, iv. 195-197, 212-218.

Religious Persecutions,
Loss of Calais, 1558.
> Bright, ii. 451-456.
> Creighton, 39-47.
> Dickens, 274-286.
> Froude, vi. 85-88, 192, 215, 256-268.
> Gardiner, ii. 424-427.
> Green, Eng. Peo., ii. 256-258.
> Green, Sh. Hist., 363-369.
> Hume, 287-290.
> Knight, iii. 66-73, 79-93, 100-106.
> Lingard, vii. 186-249.
> Yonge, iv. 204-206, 231-243, 254-263, 274-285.

ELIZABETH. 1558-1603.

Montgomery, 208-228.   Anderson, 198-216.   Towle, 206-227.

Difficulties of Position,
Religious Policy,
Strength of Parties,
Acts of Supremacy and Uniformity,
> Bright, ii. 488-495.
> Creighton, 45-52.
> Froude, vii. 5-13, 21-25, 54-58, 78-84.
> Gardiner, ii. 428-431.
> Green, Eng. Peo., ii. 295-310.
> Green, Sh. Hist., 369-379.
> Hume, 292-294.
> Knight, iii. 107-114.
> Lingard, vii. 250-268.
> Yonge, iv. 286-297.

The Tudors

Mary, Queen of Scots:

Knox and Scottish Reformation,
Mary's Character and Ability,
Reign,
Flight into England,

- Bright, ii. 495-500, 505-512.
- Creighton, 59-69, 72-82, 104, 105.
- Dickens, 288-296.
- Froude, viii. 348-379.
- Gardiner, ii. 432-440.
- Green, Eng. Peo., ii. 310-313, 330-338, 340-354, 361-364, 372-375.
- Green, Sh. Hist., 379-388.
- Hume, 294-304.
- Knight, iii. 115-128, 133-157.
- Lingard, vii. 268-307, 322-342, 347-374, viii. 1-20.
- Yonge, iv. 298-307, 341-353, v. 3-22, 39-47.

Imprisonment,
Conspiracies,
Death,

- Bright, ii. 514-525, 544-558.
- Creighton, 105-108, 166, 175-178.
- Dickens, 296-305.
- Froude, xii. 222-363.
- Gardiner, ii. 440-446, 457, 458.
- Green, Eng. Peo., ii. 375-384, 436-439.
- Green, Sh. Hist., 388-392, 415-417.
- Hume, 304-307, 310, 317-324.
- Knight, iii. 157-163, 168-174, 198-204.
- Lingard, viii. 20-57, 71-104, 162-172.
- Wheeler, 206-213.
- Yonge, v. 48-55, 83-92, 191-198, 213-237.

Essex and Ireland,

- Bright, ii. 563, 571-579.
- Creighton, 189, 190, 228-234.
- Dickens, 307-309.
- Gardiner, ii. 451-453, 475-478.
- Green, Eng. Peo., ii. 496-498.
- Green, Sh. Hist., 455-459.
- Knight, iii. 279-291.
- Towle, Ireland, 120-146.
- Yonge, v. 374-393.

Relation of England with France, Spain, and The Netherlands,

- Bright, ii. 501, 502, 512, 513, 516, 525-534, 564-566.
- Creighton, 69-72, 90-96, 113-123, 168, 173.
- Gardiner, ii. 442-444, 449, 450, 454-457.
- Green, Eng. Peo., ii. 313-315, 325-328, 337-340, 345, 346, 370, 371, 399-403, 418-429.

English History

Relation of England with France, Spain, and The Netherlands, (*Continued.*)

- Green. Sh. Hist., 411-416.
- Knight, iii. 174-178, 181-185. 238-240, 264-266.
- Lingard, vii. 308-314. 320-322, viii. 83-85, 104-108, 112-135.
- Yonge, v. 66-82, 94-131, 199-210.

Naval Enterprises of Drake, Raleigh, and others,

- Bright, ii. 554-559, 560. 572.
- Creighton, 173-181, 189-193.
- Froude, viii. 483-495, ix. 362-370. xi. 31-33. 109-112, 393-411, 418-429, xii. 161-168.
- Gardiner, ii. 446-451, 464. 489.
- Green, Eng. Peo., ii. 423-427, 432, 433.
- Hume, 312, 313. 316, 325, 326. 329.
- Lingard, viii. 274-286, ix. 164-186.
- Wheeler, 220-225.
- Yonge, v. 65, 181-190, 252, 253, 343-352.

Spanish Armada,

- Bright, ii. 559-563.
- Creasy, 239-263.
- Creighton, 181-187.
- Dickens, 305-307.
- Froude, xii. 391-544.
- Gardiner, ii. 458-464.
- Green, Eng. Peo., ii. 440-453.
- Green, Sh. Hist., 417-420.
- Hume, 325-329.
- Knight, iii. 213-237.
- Lingard, viii. 286-301.
- Wheeler, 213-219.
- Yonge, v. 258-272.

Character of Elizabeth and her Reign.

- Creighton, 68, 128-148.
- Froude, xii. 580-587.
- Gardiner, ii. 462-473.
- Green, Eng. Peo., ii. 316-323.
- Green, Sh. Hist., 370-376.
- Hume, 337.
- Lingard, viii. 416-428.
- Wheeler, 200-205.

Literature:

Sidney,

- Creighton, 213, 216.
- Green, Eng. Peo., ii. 457, 458.
- Welsh, i. 341-347.

The Tudors

Spenser
- Bright, ii. 574, 575.
- Creighton, 216-218.
- Gardiner, ii. 73, 74.
- Green, Eng. Peo., ii. 461-467.
- Green, Sh. Hist., 422-426.
- Knight, iii. 300.
- Welsh, i. 358-373.

Bacon.
- Bright, ii. 575.
- Creighton, 214, 215.
- Green, Eng. Peo., ii. 485-490.
- Welsh, i. 456-472.

Drama

Greene,
Jonson,
Marlowe,
Shakespeare.
- Bright, ii. 574.
- Creighton, 218-226.
- Green, Eng. Peo., ii. 470-485.
- Green, Sh. Hist., 428-436.
- Knight, iii. 298, 299, 301.
- Welsh, i. 313-321, 373-400, 444-456.

MRS. CHARLES: *The Schoenberg-Cotta Family.*
EBERS: *A Word; The Burgermaster's Wife.*
HENTY: *By England's Aid; Under Drake's Flag.*
KINGSLEY: *Westward Ho!*
MRS. MANNING: *Household of Sir Thomas More; Passages in the Life of the Faire Gospeller, Mrs. Anne Askew.*
MISS MUELBACH: *Henry VIII. and his Court.*
SCOTT: *The Monastery* (1559); *The Abbot* (1568); *Kenilworth* (1575).
MARK TWAIN: *The Prince and the Pauper.*
MISS YONGE: *The Dove in the Eagle's Nest; The Armourer's Prentices; Unknown to History.*
SCOTT: *Marmion; Lady of the Lake; Lay of the Last Minstrel.*
SCHILLER: *Maria Stuart.*
SHAKESPEARE: *Henry VIII.*
TENNYSON: *Queen Mary; Revenge.*

House of Stuart. 1603-1649, 1660-1714.

James I. 1603-1625.

Montgomery, 229-238.   Anderson, 219-225.   Towle, 228-233.

Great Petition,
Hampton Court
  Conference.
Gunpowder Plot,
- Bright, ii. 587-592.
- Dickens, 312-320.
- Gardiner, Eng. Hist., ii. 481-483.
- Gardiner, Puritan Rev., 13-24.
- Green, Eng. Peo., iii. 58-65.
- Green, Sh. Hist., 479-484.
- Hume, 347-350.
- Knight, iii. 314-337.
- Lingard, ix. 1-70.
- Yonge, vi. 21-47.

Divine Right of
  Kings,
Favorites,
- Bright, ii. 582-584, 597-599.
- Dickens, 320-326.
- Gardiner, Eng. Hist., ii. 484-495.
- Gardiner, Puritan Rev., 26-30.
- Green, Eng. Peo., iii. 71-74, 84-99.
- Green, Sh. Hist., 477-479, 485-488.
- Hume, 352, 353.
- Knight, iii. 341, 364-370.
- Yonge, vi. 74-82, 152-157.

American
  Colonies,
Virginia,
Pilgrims.
- Gardiner, Eng. Hist., ii. 489, 490.
- Gardiner, Puritan Rev., 85-88.
- Green, Eng. Peo., iii. 167-171.
- Green, Sh. Hist., 505-508.
- Hume, 354.
- Knight, iii. 343-346.

House of Stuart

Charles I. 1625-1649.

Montgomery, 238-247.   Anderson, 226-243.   Towle, 234-247.

Impeachment of
Buckingham,
Illegal Taxes and
forced Loans,
Petition of Right,
Monopolies,

- Bright, ii. 615-625.
- Cordery and Phillpotts, 34-47, 54, 55, 240.
- Dickens, 327-331.
- Gardiner, Eng. Hist., ii. 502-510.
- Gardiner, Puritan Rev., 54-63.
- Green, Eng. Peo., iii. 127-131, 135-138, 146-148.
- Green, Sh. Hist., 497-503, 517.
- Guizot, 15-33.
- Hume, 364-371, 394-396.
- Knight, iii. 390-404.
- Lingard, ix. 181-304.
- Macaulay, i. 66, 67.
- Yonge, vi. 103-202, 210-214, 271-273.

Wentworth,
Star Chamber,
"Thorough,"
Laud,
High Commission Court,
Ship Money,
John Hampden.

- Bright, ii. 626-640.
- Cordery and Phillpotts, 47, 48, 58-69, 72, 73.
- Dickens, 331-335.
- Gardiner, Eng. Hist., ii. 510-528.
- Gardiner, Puritan Rev., 9, 10, 74-81, 88-91, 94-98, 101-106.
- Green, Eng. Peo., iii. 150-164, 173-178, 182, 183.
- Green, Sh. Hist., 516-525, 527-531.
- Guizot, 38-42, 65-68.
- Hume, 371-376.
- Knight, iii. 409-411, 415, 423.
- Lingard, ix. 304-384.
- Macaulay, i. 67-70.
- Towle, Ireland, 161-167.
- Yonge, vi. 273-287.

Puritan Revolution:

Acts of Long
Parliament,

- Bright, ii. 644-656.
- Cordery and Phillpotts, 82-111.
- Dickens, 335-343.
- Gardiner, Eng. Hist., ii. 529-537.

English History

Acts of Long Parliament.
(Continued.)

- Gardiner, Puritan Rev., 115-130.
- Green, Eng. Peo., iii. 193-199, 209, 210.
- Green, Sh. Hist., 535-544.
- Guizot, 88-93, 100-109.
- Hume, 380-394.
- Knight, iii. 448-463, 466-476.
- Lingard, x. 1-56, 86-92, 133-139.
- Macaulay, i. 74-85.
- Wheeler, 232-243.
- Yonge, vi. 332-350, 365-375.

Civil War, 1642-1648:

Edgehill, Rise of Cromwell, Marston Moor, Naseby,

- Bright, ii. 657-686.
- Cordery and Phillpotts, 123-188, 209, 210.
- Dickens, 343-351.
- Gardiner, Eng. Hist., ii. 529-537.
- Gardiner, Puritan Rev., 130-156.
- Green, Eng. Peo., iii. 217-243.
- Green, Sh. Hist., 547-559.
- Guizot, 161-171, 183, 184, 235-241, 270-276.
- Harrison, Oliver Cromwell, 55-99, 120-125.
- Hume, 397-421.
- Knight, iv. 1-17, 29, 30, 33-48.
- Lingard, x. 64-86, 92, 93, 113-125, 152-169, 178-189.
- Macaulay, i. 88-96.
- Yonge, vii. 8-14, 42-58.

Pride's Purge, Rump Parliament, Trial and Execution of the King.

- Bright, ii. 686, 687.
- Cordery and Phillpotts, 236-247.
- Dickens, 351-355.
- Gardiner, Eng. Hist., ii. 555-560.
- Gardiner, Puritan Rev., 156-160.
- Green, Eng. Peo., iii. 253-262.
- Green, Sh. Hist., 568-572.
- Guizot, 414-436.
- Harrison, 125-129.
- Hume, 421-426.
- Knight, iv. 103-112.
- Lingard, x. 242-269.
- Macaulay, i. 96-100.
- Wheeler, 244-250.
- Yonge, vii. 110-128.

House of Stuart

COMMONWEALTH. 1649-1660.

Montgomery, 247-257.   Anderson, 243-251.   Towle, 248-252, 269.

**Cromwell in Ireland,
Cromwell in Scotland,
Battle of Worcester,
Parliaments,
Protector,
Richard Cromwell,**

- Bright, ii. 688-721.
- Cordery and Phillpotts, 281-284, 311-316, 324-327, 333-366.
- Dickens, 356-372.
- Gardiner, Eng. Hist., ii. 561-577.
- Gardiner, Puritan Rev., 160-194.
- Green, Eng. Peo., iii. 267-303, 313-319.
- Green, Sh. Hist., 572-600.
- Harrison, 130-228.
- Hume, 427-452.
- Knight, iv. 121-127, 132-140, 158-161, 182-190, 201-203, 209-211, 214-224.
- Lingard, x. 282-400, xi. 1-190.
- Macaulay, i. 101-116.
- Towle, Ireland, 178-193.
- Wheeler, 250-267.
- Yonge, vii. 144-148, 158-162, 165-168, 210-214, 226-230, 236, 237.

Milton.

- Cordery and Phillpotts, 207, 208, 259, 296, 382, 383.
- Gardiner, Eng. Hist., ii. 596, 597.
- Gardiner, Puritan Rev., 91, 92, 99, 100, 146, 147, 182, 201-204, 214.
- Green, Eng. Peo., iii. 21-23, 164, 167, 329, 376-381.
- Green, Sh. Hist., 464-467, 525-527, 600-604.
- Welsh, i. 472-495.

RESTORATION.

CHARLES II. 1660–1685.

Montgomery, 257-270.   Anderson, 251-262.   Towle, 253-262.

Punishment of Regicides, Religious Persecutions, Covenanters, Bunyan,	Bright, ii. 722-729, 732. Dickens, 372-376, 385, 386. Gardiner, ii. 578-589, 590, 596, 597. Green, Eng. Peo., iii. 354-357, 361-364, 375, 376, 398-402. Green, Sh. Hist., 467, 617-628, 640. Hale, 37-42. Hume, 453-459. Knight, iv. 244-252, 267, 268, 275, 345, 346, 366, 367. Lingard, xi. 191-242. Macaulay, i. 123-130, 138, 139, 143-145, ii. 176, 177. Welsh, ii. 45-54. Yonge, vii. 248-256, 267-275.
Royal Favorites, The Cabal,	Bright, ii. 730-734, 739, 740. Dickens, 380-392. Gardiner, ii. 593, 594, 602-605. Green, Eng. Peo., iii. 336-339, 364, 371, 386-393. Green, Sh. Hist., 630, 635-639. Hale, 20, 21. Hume, 464, 465. Knight, iv. 265, 299-307. Lingard, xi. 316-323, xii. 1-5. Macaulay, i. 164-168, 171-178. Yonge, vii. 293-300.
Plague, Fire,	Bright, ii. 738. Dickens, 376-379. Gardiner, ii. 590, 592.

Restoration

Plague,
Fire,
(Continued.)
- Green. Eng. Peo., iii. 373, 382.
- Hume, 461, 463.
- Knight, iv. 269-275, 282-288.
- Lingard, xi. 281-303.
- Yonge, vii. 281-284, 289-291.

Dutch and French Affairs,
- Bright, ii. 734-749.
- Gardiner, ii. 589, 590-593.
- Green, Eng. Peo., iii. 349, 371-375, 381-385, 394-397, 411.
- Green, Sh. Hist., 628, 629, 635-640, 646, 648, 649.
- Hale, 3-5, 33.
- Hume, 459-473.
- Knight, iv. 277-282, 297, 298, 310-313, 315-318, 324.
- Lingard, xi. 272-281, 310-315, 325-328, 334-338, xii. 11-18, 30-36, 43-46, 86-89, 98-102, 105-128.
- Macaulay, i. 149, 150, 154-163, 168-178.
- Yonge, vii. 276-281, 284-288, 291, 292, 301-328.

Plots.
- Bright, ii. 750-760.
- Dickens, 382-385.
- Gardiner, ii. 615-626.
- Green, Eng. Peo. iii. 420-424, 450, 451.
- Green, Sh. Hist., 649-652, 661.
- Hale, 21-26, 60-66.
- Hume, 476-482, 493-496.
- Knight, iv. 332-338, 345, 371-375.
- Lingard, xii. 129-172, 227-262, 316-324.
- Macaulay, i. 181-185, 208-210.
- Towle, Ireland, 194, 195.

JAMES II. 1685-1688.

Montgomery, 270-280.   Anderson, 262-269.   Towle, 263-267.

Monmouth's Rebellion,
Sedgemoor,
Bloody Assizes,
- Bright, ii. 764-768.
- Dickens, 393-399.
- Gardiner, ii. 634-638.
- Green, Eng. Peo., iv. 7-10.
- Green, Sh. Hist., 655-666.

English History

Monmouth's Rebellion, Sedgemoor, Bloody Assizes,
(*Continued.*)

- Hale, 95-102.
- Hume, 500-503.
- Knight, iv. 390-400.
- Lingard, xii. 24-68.
- Macaulay, i. 451-526.
- Wheeler, 212-278.

Popish Measures, Declaration of Indulgence, Petition and Trial of Seven Bishops,

- Bright, ii. 769-779.
- Dickens, 399-402.
- Gardiner, ii. 638-643.
- Green, Eng. Peo., iv. 13-25.
- Green, Sh. Hist., 667-672.
- Hale, 107-115, 125-129.
- Hume, 504-508.
- Knight, iv. 407-414, 418-429.
- Lingard, xii. 76-167.
- Macaulay, ii. 7-9, 66-69, 164-167, 267-305.

Invitation to William of Orange, His Coming, Flight of James.

- Bright, ii. 779-789.
- Dickens, 402-405.
- Gardiner, ii. 643-648.
- Green, Eng. Peo., iv. 25-35.
- Green, Sh. Hist., 678-681.
- Hale, 129-131, 134-152.
- Hume, 510-515.
- Knight, iv. 433-442.
- Lingard, xii. 168-236.
- Macaulay, ii. 318-321, 369-395, 428-430, 450, 460.
- Traill, 20-38.

HOUSE OF ORANGE–STUART.

WILLIAM AND MARY. 1688-1702.

Montgomery, 280-289. Anderson, 269-275. Towle, 273-285.

Bill of Rights, Mutiny Bill, Toleration Act,

- Bright, iii. 806-811.
- Gardiner, iii. 649-652.
- Green, Eng. Peo., iv. 44-47.
- Green, Sh. Hist., 682-684, 688-691.

Restoration

Bill of Rights,
Mutiny Bill,
Toleration Act,
(*Continued.*)

- Hale, 160-165.
- Hume, 523, 524, 527.
- Knight, iv. 444-447, v. 73-76.
- Lingard, xii. 236-248.
- Lecky, i. 552.
- Macaulay, ii. 509-513, iii. 34-38, 394-396.
- McCarthy, Four Georges, i. 3, 4.
- Traill, 52-55, 63-66.

Siege of Londonderry,
Battle of the Boyne,
Glencoe,

- Bright, iii. 813-836.
- Gardiner, iii. 652-657.
- Green, Eng. Peo., iv. 37-43, 50-54.
- Green, Sh. Hist., 685-694.
- Hale, 154, 155, 168-176, 181-186, 198-202.
- Hume, 525-530.
- Knight, v. 82-94, 105-112, 131-144.
- Macaulay, iii. 113-128, 179-190, 496-503, iv. 153-170.
- Towle, Ireland, 196-214.
- Traill, 67-70, 83-92, 99-103.
- Wheeler, 282-286.

Continental Wars,
Peace of Ryswick,

- Bright, iii. 836-841, 847, 856-859.
- Gardiner, iii. 657, 658, 667.
- Green, Eng. Peo., iv. 54-58, 65, 66, 72, 73.
- Green, Sh. Hist., 696-700.
- Hale, 206-219, 230-232, 237-244.
- Hume, 532, 533, 535, 536.
- Knight, v. 121-124, 147-154, 161-166, 178-181, 198-200.
- Macaulay, iv. 186-195, 209-225, 464-477, 629-643.
- Traill, 93-98, 104-108, 111-118, 147-155.

National Debt,
Bank of England.

- Bright, iii. 840, 843, 844, 852, 853.
- Gardiner, iii. 658-661.
- Green, Eng. Peo., iv. 62.
- Hale, 221, 222.
- Knight, v. 157, 158, 171.
- Macaulay, iv. 255-264, 391-403.

ANNE. 1702-1714.

Montgomery, 289-300.   Anderson, 275-280.   Towle, 284-290.

War of the Spanish Succession, Marlborough, Peace of Utrecht,

- Bright, iii. 832-834, 846, 875-921.
- Creasy, 265-288.
- Gardiner, iii. 676-685, 689-692, 696-698.
- Green, Eng. Peo., iv. 77-101.
- Green, Sh. Hist., 705-720.
- Hume, 537-539, 549-565.
- Knight, v. 259-261, 274-289, 290-310, 337-346, 364-369, 374-381.
- Lecky, i. 38-54, 106-138.
- Macaulay, ii. 197-201, iii. 346, 347, 444-448, iv. 46-51, 127-137.
- McCarthy, Four Georges, i. 22-26, 52-54, 92-95, 208-211.
- Morris, Age of Anne, 5-12, 25-29, 40-48, 56-65, 73-105, 128, 129, 132-138.
- Wheeler, 286-293.

Union of Scotland with England, 1707.

- Bright, iii. 924-928.
- Gardiner, iii. 685, 686.
- Green, Eng. Peo., iv. 90-92.
- Green, Sh. Hist., 714, 715.
- Hume, 554-556.
- Knight, v. 311-328.
- Morris, Age of Anne, 138-145.

Literature:

Pope, Swift, Defoe, Steele, Addison.

- Bright, iii. 957, 978.
- Gardiner, iii. 692-695.
- Green, Eng. Peo., iii. 326, iv. 98, 113, 114, 206-210.
- Hume, 577.
- Knight, v. 401-445.
- McCarthy, Four Georges, i. 34-48, 240-248, 299-303.
- Morris, Age of Anne, 215-231.
- Morris, Early Hanoverians, 46-48.

BLACKMORE: *Lorna Doone.*
MRS. CHARLES: *On Both Sides of the Sea; The Draytons and the Davenants.*

DOYLE: *Micah Clarke.*
HENTY: *Orange and Green ; The Cornet of Horse.*
MACDONALD: *St. George and St. Michael.*
SCOTT: *The Fortunes of Nigel ; Legend of Montrose ; Woodstock ; Peveril of the Peak ; Old Mortality ; The Pirate ; The Bride of Lammermoor ; The Black Dwarf.*
SHORTHOUSE: *John Inglesant.*
SCRIBE: *A Glass of Water.*
THACKERAY: *Henry Esmond.*
SCOTT: *Rokeby.*

English History

HOUSE OF HANOVER. 1714.

GEORGE I. 1714–1727.

Montgomery, 306-314.   Anderson, 293-295.   Towle, 291-296.

Jacobite Rebellion,
- Bright, iii. 932-938.
- Gardiner, iii. 702-706.
- Green, Eng. Peo., iv. 129, 131.
- Green, Sh. Hist., 724, 725.
- Hume, 576.
- Knight, vi. 6-22.
- McCarthy, Four Georges, i. 39, 40, 116-143.
- Morris, Early Hanoverians, 33-43.

South Sea Bubble,
- Bright, iii. 949-955.
- Gardiner, iii. 711-713.
- Green, Eng. Peo., iv. 136, 137.
- Green, Sh. Hist., 728.
- Hume, 574-576.
- Knight, vi. 39-46.
- Lecky, i. 348-350.
- McCarthy, Four Georges, i. 183-201.
- Morris, Early Hanoverians, 55-59.

Robert Walpole.
- Bright, iii. 946, 947, 955-958, 966, 967, 973-987.
- Gardiner, iii. 708-726.
- Green, Eng. Peo., iv. 126-129, 137-144, 156, 157.
- Green, Sh. Hist., 728-734.
- Hume, 574, 581, 583-585.
- Lecky, i. 351-362, 391-404, 428-432.
- McCarthy, Four Georges, i. 32-34, 165-167, 224-239, 277.
- Morris, Early Hanoverians, 59-67, 81, 82, 86-90.
- Wheeler, 294-298.

House of Hanover

GEORGE II. 1727-1760.

Montgomery, 314-322. Anderson, 295-308. Towle, 296-305.

War with Spain, War of Austrian Succession,	Bright, iii. 975, 976, 980-984, 988-999, 1010-1012. Gardiner, iii. 726-739, 743. Green, Eng. Peo., iv. 151-161, 163, 164. Green, Sh. Hist., 726-730, 734. Hume, 582, 587, 596. Knight, vi. 71-73, 93-114. Lecky, i. 414-426, 433-456, 458-466. McCarthy, Four Georges, i. 228, 296-298, ii. 147-184. Morris, Early Hanoverians, 103-143, 174-184.
Second Jacobite Rebellion,	Bright, iii. 999-1009. Gardiner, iii. 739-743. Green, Eng. Peo., iv. 161-163. Green, Sh. Hist., 743, 744. Hume, 589-596. Knight, vi. 114-118, 121-133, 155-176. Lecky, i. 456-458. McCarthy, Four Georges, ii. 199-236. Morris, 143-174. Wheeler, 305-310.
War in the East, Black Hole of Calcutta, Lord Clive,	Bright, iii. 1026, 1113-1124. Gardiner, iii. 758-764. Green, Eng. Peo., iv. 164-166, 183-185. Green, Sh. Hist., 745, 746, 753, 754. Hume, 609, 610. Knight, vi. 200-205, 222-226. Lecky, ii. 495, 496, 540-550, iii. 513-534. McCarthy, Four Georges, ii. 253-273. Wheeler, 318-324.
William Pitt (Lord Chatham),	Bright, iii. 1021, 1022, 1024, 1025, 1053, 1054. Gardiner, iii. 746-752, 766, 772-777, 787. Green, Eng. Peo., iv. 176-183, 194, 195, 212-215, 238-245, 259-261.

**William Pitt
(Lord Chatham),**
(Continued.)

- Green. Sh. Hist., 748-753, 772-774, 780, 781.
- Hume, 583, 599, 600, 613-615, 623, 624.
- Lecky, ii. 508-528, iv. 86-94.
- McCarthy, Four Georges, ii. 52-55.
- Wheeler, 311-318.

Seven Years' War in Europe and America, 1756.

- Bright, iii. 1019-1033, 1038-1041.
- Gardiner, iii. 747-756.
- Green, Eng. Peo., iv. 166-176, 185-189, 214-217.
- Green, Sh. Hist., 741, 742, 745-748, 754-764.
- Hume, 597-603.
- Knight, vi. 205-209, 213-216, 226-240.
- Lecky, ii. 482-497, 528-530, 536-540, 550-558, iii. 33-51.
- McCarthy, Four Georges, ii. 282-291.
- Wheeler, 324-329.

Methodism: Whitefield, John Wesley, Chas. Wesley.

- Bright, iii. 1015-1017.
- Gardiner, 745, 746.
- Green, Eng. Peo., iv. 145-150.
- Green, Sh. Hist., 735-739.
- Knight, vii. 121, 122.
- Lecky, ii. 577-582, 598-699.
- McCarthy, Four Georges, ii. 127-146.
- Morris, 185-190.
- Wheeler, 298-305.

GEORGE III. 1760–1820.

Montgomery, 323-344. Anderson, 308-331. Towle, 306-342.

American War: Taxation, Stamp Act, Tea Tax, Revolution,

- Bright, iii. 1045-1048, 1051, 1052, 1056, 1057, 1061, 1062, 1067-1084, 1095-1103.
- Creasy, 305-327.
- Gardiner, iii. 770-774, 777-789, 792-794, 798.
- Green, Eng. Peo., iv. 218-220, 225-238, 249-261, 266-271.
- Green, Sh. Hist., 768-772, 776-782, 785, 786.
- Hume, 612-629.

House of Hanover 63

American War :
Taxation, Stamp
Act, Tea Tax,
Revolution,
(*Continued.*)

Knight, vi. 306-314, 336-365, 383, 384, 411-416, 423-430.
Lecky, iii. 333-499, iv. 1-69, 128-163, 199-220, 266-275.
McCarthy, Four Georges, i. 310-313.
Wheeler, 324-329.

Riots,
Trial of
Warren Hastings,

Bright, iii. 1092-1094, 1124-1131, 1139-1141, 1156, 1164.
Gardiner, iii. 789-792, 801-811.
Green, Eng. Peo., iv. 275, 276.
Green, Sh. Hist., 782-785, 795, 796.
Hume, 625-627, 637-640.
Knight, vi. 400-410, viii. 82, 83.
Lecky, iii. 143-150, 163, 164, 283, 553-568.
Wheeler, 335-341.

Freedom of Press,
Prison Reforms,
Slave Trade,

Bright, iii. 1043, 1044, 1062, 1063, 1142, 1271, 1272.
Green, Eng. Peo., iv. 220-225, 248, 249, 273-277.
Gardiner, iii. 779, 780, 823.
Green, Sh. Hist., 767, 768, 774-776, 796, 797.
Hume, 610, 611, 671.
Knight, vii. 117-120, 212, viii. 85-90, 193, 194.
Lecky, ii. 13-18, iii. 78-89, 139-142, 247-252, 278-289.
Mackenzie, 79, 80, 85, 86.
Martineau, 208-212, 231-235.

War with France,
Waterloo,

Bright, iii. 1108-1110, 1165-1177, 1189-1198, 1220-1224, 1231-1242, 1253-1257, 1262-1266, 1285-1321, 1339-1248.
Creasy, 346-364.
Gardiner, iii. 788-798, 834-840, 843-875.
Green, Eng. Peo., iv. 296, 297, 302-322, 328-340, 352-368, 371-389.
Green, Sh. Hist., 805-811, 818-827, 834-836.
Hume, 644-693.
Knight, vii. 346-360, 397-390, 401-408, 441-450, 499-508, 562-571, viii. 29-37.

English History

War with France, Waterloo, (*Continued.*)

> Lecky, iv. 262-266.
> Mackenzie, 32-61.
> Martineau, 49-58, 72-92, 138-157, 161-186, 204-207, 216-223, 261-286, 491-529.
> Wheeler, 341-356.

The Younger Pitt,

> Bright, iii. 1132-1139, 1143, 1144, 1156, 1157, 1177, 1243-1247, 1257-1259, 1266.
> Gardiner, iii. 799-801, 806-812, 819, 822, 825, 827-830, 842, 843, 855.
> Green, Eng. Peo., iv. 284-296, 344-347, 349, 350.
> Green, Sh. Hist., 790-795.
> Knight, vii. 139-155.
> Lecky, iv. 320-336.
> Martineau, 32-42, 51, 52, 99-112, 157-161.

Second War with America,

> Bright, iii. 1325-1328.
> Gardiner, iii. 872, 873.
> Green, Eng. Peo., iv. 378, 379, 383, 384.
> Green, Sh. Hist., 832-834.
> Hume, 689.
> Knight, vii. 544, 545, viii. 1-19.
> Mackenzie, 412-414.
> Martineau, 123-131, 287-315.

Union with Ireland.

> Bright, iii. 1209-1219.
> Gardiner, iii. 831-834, 841, 842.
> Green, Eng. Peo., iv. 337, 338.
> Green, Sh. Hist., 811-815.
> Hume, 655-657.
> Martineau, 24-29, 58-72.
> Towle, Ireland, 252-259.

GEORGE IV. 1820–1830.

Montgomery 344-349. Anderson, 344-348. Towle, 342-346.

Legislative Reform, Repeal of Test and Corporation Acts, Catholic Emancipation.

> Bright, iii. 1389, 1390, 1401-1410.
> Gardiner, iii. 875-880, 885, 886, 894-898.
> Hume, 698-701.
> Knight, viii. 232-240.
> McCarthy, Epoch of Ref., 2, 3, 21-25.
> Green, Sh. Hist., 838-840.
> Mackenzie, 112, 113.

House of Hanover

WILLIAM IV. 1830-1837.

Montgomery, 349-357. Anderson, 349-351. Towle, 346-352.

Reform Bill,
- Bright, iii. 1423-1434.
- Gardiner, iii. 901-905.
- Hume, 702-705.
- Knight, viii. 270-285, 293, 299, 300.
- McCarthy, Epoch of Ref., 25-83.
- Mackenzie, 100-109.

Emancipation of Slaves, 1833, Poor Law.
- Bright, iii. 1442-1445, 1451-1454.
- Gardiner, iii. 910, 911.
- Hume, 705, 706.
- Knight, vii. 466-468, 478, viii. 327-32.
- Mackenzie, 80-82, 116, 119-121.
- McCarthy, Epoch of Ref., 83-98, 124-130.

Literature:

Byron, Burns, Coleridge, Goldsmith, Johnson, Lamb, Macaulay Scott, Shelley, Wordsworth.
- Gardiner, iii. 887-890.
- Knight, vii. 83-96, viii. 111-129.
- Welsh, ii. 274-355.

Discoveries, Inventions.
- Gardiner, iii. 813-818, 905-909, 940.
- Green, iv. 377-384.
- Knight, vii. 40-63, viii. 129-132, 258-262.
- Martineau, 521-531.

MRS. CHARLES: *Against the Stream.*
COOPER: *Wing and Wing.*
DICKENS: *Barnaby Rudge; Tale of Two Cities.*
HENTY: *Bonnie Prince Charlie; Held Fast for England; The Bravest of the Brave; The Young Buglers; With Clive in India.*
SCOTT: *Rob Roy* (1715); *Heart of Midlothian; Waverley* (1745); *Guy Mannering; Redgauntlet; Antiquary.*
THACKERAY: *The Virginians.*

Victoria. 1837–

Montgomery, 357-363. Anderson, 351-376. Towle, 352-366.

Rise of Chartists,
- Bright, iv. 44-46, 79, 80, 87, 91-93, 176-178.
- Gardiner, iii. 922-924.
- Hume, 708-711.
- Knight, viii. 417, 418, 421-423.
- Mackenzie, 155-158.
- McCarthy, H. O. O. T., i. 70-88, 292-302.
- McCarthy, Epoch of Ref., 165, 166.

Corn Laws,
Irish Famine,
Free Trade,
- Bright, iv. 78-86, 93, 121, 128-138, 156-161, 219.
- Gardiner, iii. 924-939.
- Green, Sh. Hist., 841.
- Hume, 708-711.
- Knight, viii. 501, 513, 517, 525-528, 535-539, 547-551.
- Mackenzie, 126-136.
- McCarthy, H. O. O. T., i. 216-256.
- McCarthy, Epoch of Ref., 175-193.
- Towle, Ireland, 267-272.

Crimean War, 1854,
- Bright, iv. 243-286.
- Gardiner, iii. 943-948.
- Green, Sh. Hist., 842.
- Hume, 713-717.
- Mackenzie, 159-176.
- McCarthy, H. O. O. T., i. 433-524.
- McCarthy, Epoch of Ref., 210, 211.
- Wheeler, 360-364.

War in India,
- Bright, iv. 292-328.
- Gardiner, iii. 948-955.
- Green, Sh. Hist., 842, 843.
- Hume, 717-721.
- Knight, viii. 451-461, 543-545.
- Mackenzie, 224-248.
- McCarthy, H. O. O. T., ii. 33-78.
- Wheeler, 364-369.

War in America,	Bright, iv. 372-385. 490, 491. Gardiner, iii. 958-960. Hume, 723, 779, 780. Mackenzie, 419-428. McCarthy, H. O. O. T., ii. 190-228.
Reform Bill,	Bright, iv. 349-352, 419, 428. Gardiner, iii. 961, 962. Hume, 726, 727. Knight, viii. 270-285, 293-300. Mackenzie, 103-109. McCarthy, H. O. O. T., ii. 351-370.
Land Act, Education Bill.	Bright, iv. 454-466. Gardiner, iii. 962, 963. Hume, 727. McCarthy, H. O. O. T., ii. 471-487. Towle, Ireland, 280-294.

Literature

Bulwer, Browning, Mrs. Browning, Carlyle, Dickens, Geo. Eliot, Mill, Tennyson, Thackeray, Tyndall.	Gardiner, iii. 940-943. Knight, viii. 467-485. McCarthy, H. O. O. T., i. 524-559, ii. 629-656. Welsh, ii. 368-370, 427-501.

INDEX

A

Ability of Mary Stuart, 47.
Act, Land, 67.
Act, Toleration, 57.
Acts of Long Parliament, 51.
Acts of Supremacy and Uniformity, 44, 46.
Addison, 58.
Agincourt, 38.
Agricola, Governm't of, 10.
Alfred, Army of, 15.
Alfred, Character of, 16.
Alfred, Childhood of, 14.
Alfred, Laws of, 15.
Alfred, Navy of, 15.
Alfred, Palaces of, 15.
Alfred, Strongholds of, 15.
Alfred, Youth of, 14.
Alliances of Henry VII., Foreign, 42.
Alliance, Austrian, 43.
America, Seven Years' War in Europe and, 62.
America, War in, 67.
American Colonies, 50.
American War, 62, 63, 64.
Ancient England, 9.
Angevin Marriage, 25.
Angevins, 26.
Anne, 58.
Arc, Joan of, 39.
Archbishop Becket, 26.
Armada, Spanish, 48.
Articles, Thirty-nine, 45.
Arthur, King, 12.
Assize of Clarendon, 26.
Assizes, Bloody, 55.
Attack on Druids, 10.
Augustine, 13.

Austrian Alliance, 43.
Austrian Succession, War of, 61.

B

Bacon, 49.
Bæda, 13.
Banishment of Jews, 30.
Bank of England, 57.
Barons' Wars, 30.
Battle of the Boyne, 57.
Battle of Spurs, 36.
Battle of the Standard, 25.
Battle of Worcester, 53.
Becket, 26.
Becket, Condemnation of, 27.
Becket, Exile and Death of, 27.
Bill, Education, 67.
Bill, Mutiny, 56.
Bill, Reform, 65, 67.
Bill of Rights, 56.
Bishops, Trial of Seven, 56.
Black Death, 33.
Black Hole of Calcutta, 61.
Black Prince in Castile, 34.
Bloody Assizes, 50.
Boadicea, Revolt of, 10.
Book, Domesday, 22.
Bosworth Field, 40.
Boy Kings, Six, 16.
Boyne, Battle of, 57.
Bretigny, Treaty of, 33.
Browning, 67.
Browning, Mrs., 67.
Bruce, Robert, 31.
Bubble, South Sea, 60.
Buckingham, Impeachment of, 51.

Bulwer, 67.
Bunyan, 54.
Burns, 65.
Byron, 65.

C

Cabal, The, 54.
Cade's Rebellion, 39.
Cædmon, 13.
Cæsar, 9.
Calais, 33.
Calais, Loss of, 46.
Calcutta, Black Hole of, 61.
Canute, 17.
Carlyle, 67.
Castile, Black Prince in, 33.
Castles, 22.
Catherine, Divorce of, 44.
Catholic Emancipation, 64.
Chamber, Star, 42, 51.
Changes, Henry's Religious, 45.
Character of Alfred, 16.
Character of Edward I., 31.
Character of Edward III., and Reign, 34.
Character of Elizabeth, and Reign, 48.
Character of English Conquest, 12.
Character of Henry II., 28.
Character of Mary, Queen of Scots, 47.
Character of Norman Conquest, 23.
Character of William the Conqueror, 23.
Character of William Rufus' Reign, 23.
Charta, Magna, 29.

Charter of Henry I., 24.
Chartists, Rise of, 66.
Charles I., 51.
Charles II., 54.
Charles V., 43.
Charles Wesley, 62.
Chatham, Lord, 61.
Chaucer, 35.
Childhood of Alfred, 14.
Churches, 22.
Church, Reforms in State and, 31.
Christianity, Coming of, 13.
Civil War, 25, 27, 52.
Clarendon, Constitutions of, 26.
Clarendon, Assize of, 26.
Claudius, Emperor, 10.
Clive, Lord, 61.
Coleridge, 65.
Colonies, American, 50.
Coming of Christianity, 13.
Coming of William of Orange, 56.
Commerce, Rise of English, 33.
Commons, House of, 30.
Commonwealth, 53.
Condemnation of Becket, 27.
Conference, Hampt'n Court 50.
Confessor, Edward the, 18.
Conquest, English, 12.
Conquest, Norman, 20.
Conquest, Norman, Results of, 23.
Conquest, Roman, 9.
Conspiracies and Revolts, 37.
Conspiracies of Mary Stuart, 47.
Constitutions of Clarendon, 26.
Contest with Church, 29.
Continental Wars, 57.

Continuation of Wars of Roses, 40.
Corn Laws, 66.
Corporation Act, Repeal of, 64.
Court, High Commis'n, 51.
Covenanters, 54.
Cranmer, 45.
Crécy, 33.
Crimean War, 66.
Cromwell in Ireland, 53.
Cromwell in Scotland, 53.
Cromwell, Rise of, 52.
Cromwell, Richard, 53.
Cromwell, Thomas, 44.
Cross, Neville's, 32.
Crowning of William the Conqueror, 21.
Crusade, First, 24.
Curfew, 22.

D

Danish Invasions, 14.
Danish Line, 17.
Death of Becket, 27.
Death of Mary Stuart, 47.
Death, Black, 33.
Debt, National, 57.
Declaration of Indulgence, 56.
Defoe, 58.
Deposition of Edward II., 32.
Deposition of Richard II., 35.
Dickens, 67.
Difficulties of Elizabeth's position, 46.
Discoveries, 42, 65.
Divine Right of Kings, 50.
Divorce of Henry VIII., 44.
Domesday Book, 22.
Drake, Naval Enterprises of, 48.
Drama, 49.
Druids, Attack on, 10.

Dunstan, 16.
Dutch and French Affairs, 55.

E

East, War in, 61.
Edgehill, 52.
Education Bill, 67.
Edward I., 30.
Edward II., 31.
Edward II., Depos'n of, 32.
Edward III., 32.
Edward IV., 40.
Edward V., 40.
Edward VI., 45.
Edward the Confessor, 18.
Effects of Black Death, 33.
Effect of Wars, 41.
Egbert, 13.
Eliot, George, 67.
Elizabeth, 46.
Elizabeth, Character of, 48.
Emancipation, Catholic, 64.
Emancipation of Slaves, 65.
Emperor Claudius, 10.
England, Ancient, 9.
England, Bank of, 57.
England, Feudalism in, 22.
England, Flight of Mary to, 47.
England, Reformation in, 45.
England, Relation of France, Spain, and Netherlands with, 47.
England, Resistance of, 21.
England, Union of Scotland with, 58.
English Commerce, Rise of, 33.
English Conquest, 12.
English, King of, 13.
English Line, 17.
Enterprises, Naval, 48.
Essex and Ireland, 47.
Europe, Seven Years' War in, 62.
Evesham, 30.

Index

Execution of Charles I., 52.
Execution of More and Fisher, 44.
Exile of Becket, 27.

F

Fall of Wolsey, 44.
Famine, Irish, 66.
Favorites, 50.
Favorites, New, 32.
Favorites, Royal, 54.
Feudalism in England, 22.
Feudalism in England under William, 22.
Field, Bosworth, 40.
Fire, Great, 54.
First Battles of War of Roses, 39.
First Crusade, 24.
Fisher, Execution of, 44.
Flight of James, 56.
Flight of Mary Stuart, 47.
Flodden, 43.
Forced Loans, 51.
Foreign Alliances, 42.
Forest, New, 22.
Forts, 11.
France, Relation of England with, 47.
France, War with, 38, 64.
Freedom of the Press, 63.
Free Trade, 66.
French Affairs, 54.
French Possessions, Loss of, 34, 39.
French War, Causes of, 33.

G

Gaveston, Piers, 31.
George I., 60.
George II., 61.
George III., 62.
George IV., 64.
George Eliot, 67.
Germany, Reform in, 45.

Glencoe, 57.
Godwin, 17.
Goldsmith, 65.
Good Parliament, 34.
Government of Agricola, 10.
Government of England, 12.
Grey, Lady Jane, 45.
Greatness, Wolsey's, 43.
Great Petition, 50.
Greene, 49.
Gregory, 13.
Gunpowder Plot, 50.
Guthrum, 15.

H

Hadrian, Wall of, 10.
Hampden, John, 51.
Hampton Court Conference, 50.
Hanover, House of, 60.
Hardicanute, 17.
Harfleur, 38.
Harold, 17, 18.
Hastings, 16.
Hastings, Warren, 63.
Henry I., 24.
Henry II., 26.
Henry III., 29.
Henry IV., 37.
Henry V., 37.
Henry VI., 38.
Henry VII., 42.
Henry VIII., 43.
Henry's Religious Changes, 45.
High Commission Court, 51.
Hole of Calcutta, Black, 61.
House of Commons, 30.
House of Hanover, 60.
House of Lancaster, 37.
Houses of Lancaster and York, 37.
House of Orange-Stuart, 56.
House of Stuart, 50.
House of York, 40.

I

Illegal Taxes, 51.
Impeachment of Buckingham, 51.
Imprisonment of Mary Stuart, 47.
Improvements, 15.
Independence, Scotland regains its, 32.
India, War in, 66.
Indulgence, Declaration of, 56.
Infidels, Zeal against, 28.
Inhabitants, Original, 9.
In Normandy, William, 20.
Introduction of Printing, 40.
Invasions, Danish, 14.
Invasions, Roman, 9.
Inventions, 65.
Invitation to William of Orange, 56.
Ireland, 27.
Ireland, Cromwell in, 53.
Ireland, Essex and, 47.
Ireland, Union with, 64.
Irish Famine, 66.

J

Jack Cade's Rebellion, 39.
Jacobite Rebellion, 60, 61.
James I., 50.
James II., 55.
James II., Flight of, 56.
Jane Grey, Lady, 45.
Jews, Banishment of, 30.
Joan of Arc, 38.
John, 28.
John Hampden, 51.
John Wesley, 62.
Johnson, 65.
Jonson, 49.

K

King, 12.
King Arthur, 12.

King of English, 13.
King-Maker, Warwick, 40.
Kings, Divine Right of, 50.
Kings, Six Boy, 16.
Knox, 47.

L

Lady Jane Grey, 45.
Lamb, 65.
Lancaster, House of, 37.
Lancaster a n d Y o r k, Houses of, 37.
Land Act, 67.
Langland, William, 36.
Langton, Stephen, 29.
Language of Ancient England, 11.
Language, State of, 35.
Latimer, 45.
Laud, 51.
Law, Poor, 65.
Laws of Alfred, 15.
Laws, Corn, 66.
Learning, New, 42.
Legislative Reform, 64.
Lewes, 30.
Life of Ancient England, Mode of, 9.
Line, Danish, 17.
Line, English, 17.
Literary Work of Alfred, 15.
Literature, 35, 48, 58.
Loans, Forced, 51.
Lollards, 35, 37.
London Tower, 22.
Londonderry, Siege of, 57.
Long Parliament, Acts of, 52.
Lord Chatham, 61.
Lord Clive, 61.
Loss of Calais, 46.
Loss of French Possessions, 34, 39.
Loss of Normandy, 28.
Luther, Martin, 45.

M

Macaulay, 65.
Mad Parliament, 29.
Magna Charta, 29.
Marlborough, 58.
Marlowe, 49.
Marriage, Angevin, 25.
Marriage of Henry I., 24.
Marston Moor, 52.
Martin Luther, 45.
Mary, 46.
Mary Stuart, 47.
Mary, Ability of, 47.
Mary, Character of, 47.
Mary, Conspiracies of, 47.
Mary, Death of, 47.
Mary, Flight of, 47.
Mary, Imprisonment of, 47.
Mary, Reign of, 47.
Mary, William and, 56.
Measures, Popish, 56.
Methodism, 62.
Mill, 67.
Milton, 53.
Mode of Life in Ancient England, 9.
Model Parliament, 31.
Monasteries, Suppression of, 44.
Money, Ship, 51.
Monmouth's Rebellion, 55.
Monopolies, 51.
Montford, Simon de, 29.
More, Execution of, 44.
Mutiny Bill, 56.

N

Naseby, 52.
National Debt, 57.
Naval Enterprises, 46.
Navy of Alfred, 15.
Netherlands, Relation of England with, 47.
Neville's Cross, 32.
New Favorites, 32.

New Forest, 22.
New Learning, 42.
New Tax, 34.
Norman Conquest, 20.
Normandy, Loss of, 28.
Normandy, William in, 20.

O

Orange, Invitation to William of, 56.
Orange-Stuart, House of, 56.
Original Inhabitants, 9.
Orleans, 38.
Oldcastle, Sir John, 37.

P

Palaces, 15.
Parliament, Acts of Long, 52.
Parliament, Good, 34.
Parliament, Mad, 29.
Parliament, Model, 31.
Parliament, Rump, 52.
Parliament, Subjection of, 44.
Parliaments of Commonwealth, 53.
Parties, Strength of, 46.
Peace of Ryswick, 57.
Peace of Utrecht, 58.
Persecution of Lollards, 37.
Persecutions, Religious, 46, 54.
Petition, Great, 50.
Petition of Right, 51.
Petition and Trial of Seven Bishops, 56.
Philip II., 46.
Piers Gaveston, 31.
Pilgrims, 50.
Pitt, William, 61.
Pitt, The Younger, 64.
Plague, 54.
Plantagenets, 26.
Plautius, 10.
Plots, 55.

Index 73

Poictiers, 33.
Poor Law, 65.
Pope, 58.
Popish Measures, 56.
Position, Difficulties of Elizabeth's, 46.
Possessions, Loss of French, 34, 39.
Prayer Book, 45.
Press, Freedom of, 63.
Pretenders, Two, 42.
Pride's Purge, 52.
Prince, Black, 34.
Printing, Introduction of, 40.
Prison Reforms, 63.
Protector, 53.
Punishment of Regicides, 54.
Puritan Revolution, 51.

Q
Quarrel with Robert, 24.
Queen of Scots, Mary, 47.

R
Raleigh, Naval Enterprises of, 48.
Rebellion, Jack Cade's, 39.
Rebellion, Jacobite, 60, 61.
Rebellion, Monmouth's, 55.
Reforms, 26.
Reforms in State and Church, 31.
Reforms, Prison, 63.
Reform Bill, 65, 67.
Reform, Legislative, 64.
Reformation, 45.
Reformation, Scottish, 47.
Regicides, Punishment of, 54.
Reign of Edward III., Character of, 34.
Reign of Elizabeth, Character of, 48.
Reign of Mary Stuart, 47.

Reign of William Rufus, Character of, 23.
Relation of England with France, Spain, and Netherlands, 47.
Religion of Early England, 11.
Religion of Original Inhabitants, 9.
Religious Changes of Henry VIII., 45.
Religious Persecutions, 46.
Religious Policy of Elizabeth, 46.
Renewal of War with France, 38.
Repeal of Test and Corporation Acts, 64.
Resistance of England, 21.
Restoration of Stuarts, 54.
Results of Norman Conquest, 23.
Results of Suppression of Monasteries, 44.
Revolts, 41.
Revolts and Conspiracies, 37.
Revolt of Boadicea, 10.
Revolution, 62.
Revolution, Puritan, 51.
Richard I., 28.
Richard II., 34.
Richard III., 41.
Richard Cromwell, 53.
Rights, Bill of, 56.
Right of Kings, Divine, 50.
Right, Petition of, 51.
Riots, 63.
Rise of Chartists, 66.
Rise of Cromwell, 52.
Rise of English Commerce, 33.
Rise of Wolsey, 43.
Robert Bruce, 31.
Robert, Quarrel with, 24.

Robert Walpole, 60.
Roman Conquests, 9.
Rome, Separation of Church from, 44.
Roses, Wars of, 39.
Rouen, Siege of, 38.
Royal Favorites, 54.
Rufus, William, 23.
Rump Parliament, 52.
Ryswick, Peace of, 57.

S
Scotland, 31.
Scotland and England, Union of, 58.
Scotland, Cromwell in, 53.
Scotland Regains its Independence, 32.
Scotland, War with, 32.
Scottish Reformation, 47.
Scott, 65.
Second Jacobite Rebellion, 61.
Second War in America, 64.
Sedgemoor, 55.
Senlac, 20.
Separation of Church from Rome, 44.
Settlement of England, 12.
Seven Bishops, Trial of, 56.
Seven Years' War in Europe and America, 62.
Severus, 10.
Shakespeare, 49.
Shelley, 65.
Ship Money, 51.
Sidney, 49.
Siege of Londonderry, 57.
Siege of Rouen, 38.
Simon de Montford, 29.
Sir John Oldcastle, 37.
Six Boy Kings, 16.
Slave Trade, 63.
Slaves, Emancipation of, 65

Index

Sluys, 33.
South Sea Bubble, 60.
Spain, Relation of England with, 47.
Spain, War with, 61.
Spanish Armada, 48.
Spanish Succession, War of, 58.
Spenser, 49.
Spurs, Battle of, 43.
Stamp Act, 62.
Standard, Battle of, 25.
Star Chamber, 42, 51.
State of Language, 35.
State, Reforms in, 31.
Steele, 58.
Stephen, 25.
Stephen Langton, 29.
Strength of Parties, 46.
Strongholds, 15.
Stuart, House of, 50.
Subjection of Parliament, 44.
Succession, Spanish, 58.
Succession, War of Austrian, 61.
Suetonius, 10.
Suppression of Monasteries, 44.
Supremacy, Act of, 44, 46.
Sweyn, 17.
Swift, 58.

T

Taxation, 62.
Taxes, Illegal, 51.
Tax, New, 34.
Tax, Tea, 62.
Tennyson, 67.
Test Act, Repeal of, 64.
Thackeray, 67.
Thirty-nine Articles, 45.
Thomas à Becket, 26.
Thomas Cromwell, 44.
"Thorough," 51.
Toleration Act, 56.
Tower of London, 22.
Trade, Free, 66.
Trade, Slave, 63.
Treaty of Bretigny, 33.
Treaty of Troyes, 38.
Treaty of Wedmore, 15.
Trial of Charles I., 52.
Trial of Seven Bishops, 56.
Trouble with France, 30.
Tudors, 42.
Two Pretenders, 42.
Tyler, Wat, 34.
Tyndale, 45.
Tyndall, 67.

U

Uniformity, Act of, 46.
Union of Scotland with England, 58.
Union of Ireland with England, 64.
Utrecht, Peace of, 58.

V

Victoria, 66.
Virginia, 50.

W

Wallace, William, 31.
Wall of Hadrian, 10.
Walpole, Robert, 60.
War, Causes of French, 33.
War, Crimean, 66.
War, Civil, 25, 27, 52.
War, Continental, 57.
War, Continuation of, 40.
War, Effects of, 41.
War in America, 67.
War in the East, 61.
War in Europe and America, 62.
War in India, 67.
War of Austrian Succession, 61.
Barons' Wars, 30.
Wars of Roses, 39.
War of Spanish Succession, 58.
War with America, 62, 64.
War with France, 38, 63.
War with Scotland, 32.
War with Spain, 61.
War, Renewal of, 38.
Warren Hastings, 63.
Warwick, King Maker, 40.
Waterloo, 63.
Wat Tyler, 34.
Wedmore, Treaty of, 15.
Welsh Campaign, 30.
Wentworth, 51.
Wesley, Charles, 62.
Wesley, John, 62.
Whitefield, 62.
William the Conqueror, 20.
William, Character of, 23.
William, Crowning of, 21.
William Langland, 36.
William IV., 65.
William and Mary, 56.
William of Orange, Invitation to, 56.
William Pitt, 61.
William Rufus, 23.
Wolsey's Rise and Greatness, 43.
Wolsey's Fall, 44.
Worcester, Battle of, 53.
Wordsworth, 65.
Wycliffe, 35.

Y

Younger Pitt, The, 64.
Youth of Alfred, 14.
York, House of, 40.
York, Houses of Lancaster and, 37.

Z

Zeal of Richard I. against Infidels, 28.

BULFINCH'S MYTHOLOGY

THE AGE OF FABLE
OR
BEAUTIES OF MYTHOLOGY

By **THOMAS BULFINCH**   Revised by Rev. **E. E. HALE**

A new and enlarged edition. The edition of 1894 contains 568 pages, including a sketch of the history of Greek sculpture, and one hundred and forty-two Illustrations connecting art with mythology. It also states where the original of each Illustration is located. Small 8vo Price cloth $2.50

THE AGE OF CHIVALRY
OR
LEGENDS OF KING ARTHUR

"Stories of the Round Table" "The Crusaders" "Robin Hood" etc.

By **THOMAS BULFINCH**   Revised by Rev. **E. E. HALE**

A new, enlarged, and revised edition Illustrated Small 8vo
Price cloth $2.50

LEGENDS OF CHARLEMAGNE
OR
ROMANCE OF THE MIDDLE AGES

STORIES OF PALADIN AND SARACEN

By **THOMAS BULFINCH**

Illustrated Small 8vo Price cloth $2.50

CATALOGUES MAILED FREE

Sent by mail, postpaid on receipt of price by

LEE AND SHEPARD BOSTON

BOOKS FOR EDUCATORS

Methods of Instruction and Organization in the Schools of Germany

By JOHN T. PRINCE, Mass. State Board of Education. $1.00 net. Cloth. Mailing price, $1.15.

A helpful and suggestive work. Mr. Prince has aimed to give the important feature of organization, and such methods observed by him as he thinks will be most useful for American teachers to know. In methods he devotes a chapter each to "Observation Lessons and Elementary Science;" "Reading;" "Language;" "Geography and History;" "Arithmetic;" "Drawing, manual-training," etc. The chapters on organization are full of interest; and the final chapter of all, a comparison between German and American schools, sums up the author's views. — *Society of Pedagogy, N.Y.*

The Spirit of the New Education

By LOUISA PARSONS HOPKINS, Supervisor of Boston Public Schools. Author of "How Shall my Child be Taught," "Observation Lessons in the Primary Schools," etc. Cloth, $1.50.

The addresses in this work have an underlying unity of thought, represent advanced theories, and afford high ideals for the development of character and the training of the young. The earnestness and sincerity of the author are undeniable, and she presents her ideas vigorously, and with a strong flavor of discussion. Manual training, the kindergarten, physical training, elementary science, the public school curriculum, moral education, women's work in education, are among the many subjects treated, with a clearness and emphasis that make a lasting impression. — *Boston Times.*

Matter, Ether, and Motion
The Factors and Relations of Physical Science

By Prof. A. E. DOLBEAR, author of "The Telephone," "The Art of Projecting," etc. Price, $2.00.

Professor A. E. Dolbear has done a valuable service to students of the various branches of physical science by putting together in the volume the latest conclusions of research and speculation concerning the molecular phenomena and the mechanical relations upon which they are based.

Professor Dolbear is a clear thinker, and his views, often characterized by great boldness and cogency of reasoning, are expressed with a lucidity and freedom from technical phraseology that render them well within the intellectual grasp of most educated readers. On the whole, it is safe to say that the mechanical theory of the universe has never before been presented in a form so definite and convincing.

Handbook of School Gymnastics of the Swedish System

By BARON NILS POSSE. Cloth. Illustrated. 50 cents net. Mailing price, 55 cents.

Baron Nils Posse has condensed the theory of Swedish gymnastics for schools in a brief essay, and, by an ingenious use of abbreviations, has compressed 100 tables of exercises into a miraculously small space, which will be found of great value by all properly taught teachers. Indeed, instructors of his system can scarcely dispense with the little volume, and all teachers and all pupils in normal schools should be provided with it. — *Boston Herald.*

Any of the above sent by mail on receipt of price.

LEE AND SHEPARD   PUBLISHERS   BOSTON

www.ingramcontent.com/pod-product-compliance
Lightning Source LLC
Chambersburg PA
CBHW022145090426
42742CB00010B/1399